BEYOND
CODEPENDENCY

BEYOND
CODEPENDENCY

And Getting Better All the Time

Melody Beattie

1949-1999
HAZELDEN

Rebuilding Lives, Restoring Families,
Building Communities

 **HAZELDEN**®

INFORMATION & EDUCATIONAL SERVICES

Editor's Note:
   The following publishers have generously given permission to use extended quotations from copyrighted works: From "To Graduates: March On, Make Mistakes," by Ellen Goodman. Copyright 1988, published by the Boston Globe Newspaper Company/Washington Post Writers Group. Reprinted with permission. From charter statement, published by National Association for Children of Alcoholics. Reprinted with permission. From *Scripts People Live*, by Claude M. Steiner. Copyright 1974 by Grove Press. Reprinted with permission. From *Games People Play* by Eric Berne, M.D. Copyright 1964, by Random House, Inc. From *Why Am I Afraid to Tell You Who I Am?* by John Powell, S.J. Copyright 1969, by Tabor Publishing, 25115 Avenue Stanford, Valencia, CA 91355. Reprinted with permission. From Bloom County, by Berke Breathed. Copyright 1988, Washington Post Writers Group. Reprinted by permission. From *Facing Shame: Families in Recovery*, by Merle A. Fossum and Marilyn J. Mason, by permission of W.W. Norton & Company, Inc. Copyright © 1986 by Merle A. Fossum and Marilyn J. Mason. From *You Can Heal Your Life* © 1987, by Louise Hay. Used by permission. Hay House. From "Donna Wallace on empowering ACOAs at work," by Kathleen Lindstron. Copyright May 1988 from *The Phoenix*. Reprinted with permission. From "Rokelle Lerner: ACA's, Intimacy and Play" by Ann Jeffries. Copyright October 1988 from *The Phoenix*. Reprinted with permission. From *GIFT FROM THE SEA*, by Anne Morrow Lindbergh. Copyright 1955 from Pantheon Books, a Division of Random House, Inc. From "Messages For Your Most Important Reader" by Lawrence Block. Copyright June 1988 from *Writers Digest* magazine. Reprinted with permission. From *Diagnosing and Treating Co-Dependence* by Timmen L. Cermak. Copyright 1986 from Johnson Institute. Reprinted with permission. From *The Rose* byAmanda McBroom. © 1979 Warner-Tamerlane Publishing Corp. All rights reserved. Used by permission. From *Shamed Faced* by Stephanie E. Copyright 1986 by Hazelden Educational Materials. Reprinted with permission. From *Andy Capp* by Reginald Smythe. Copyright 1988 from Syndication International LTD. Reprinted with permission. From *Beyond Cinderella: How to Find and Marry the Man You Want*, by Nita Tucker and Debra Feinstein. Copyright 1987 by St. Martin's Press, Inc., New York. Reprinted with permission. From "Healing Your Life with Louise Hay," by Carolyn Rueben. Copyright 1988 by *East West the Journal of Natural Health and Living*. Reprinted with permission. From *Women Who Love Too Much*, by Robin Norwood. Copyright 1985 Robin Norwood, Jeremy P. Tarcher, Inc. Reprinted with permission. From *Loving Men for All the Right Reasons: Women's Patterns of Intimacy*, by Yehuda Nir, M.D. and Bonnie Maslin, M.D. Copyright 1982 from Dell Publishing Co., Inc. Reprinted with permission from authors. From *Men Who Can't Love*, by Steven Carter and Julia Sokol. Copyright © 1987 by Steven Carter and Julia Sokol Coopersmith. Reprinted by permission of the publisher, M. Evans and Company, Inc. From *Choosing Lovers*, by Martin Blinder, M.D. Copyright 1988 from Glenbridge Publishing. Reprinted with permission of the author. From *Co-Dependency, An Emerging Issue*, by Robert Subby, et al. Copyright 1984 by Health Communications. Reprinted with permission. From *Struggle for Intimacy*, by Janet Geringer Woititz. Copyright 1985 by Health Communications. Reprinted with permission. From *Hardball*, by Christopher Matthews. Copyright 1988 by Simon and Schuster. Reprinted with permission. From *A Road Less Traveled*, by M. Scott Peck. Copyright 1980 by Simon and Schuster. Reprinted with permission. From *Treating the Codependent: Diagnosis, Recovery and Relapse Prevention Planning* (unpublished but copyrighted by Cenaps Corporation, workshop handout), by Terence T. Gorski and Merlene M. Miller, Hazel Crest, Illinois, 1984. Reprinted with permission.

Dedication

One night, in a dream, I saw a group of people. These people were deserving, lovable people. The problem was, they didn't know it. They were stuck, confused — reacting to some crazy stuff that happened long ago.

They were running around in adult bodies, but in many ways they were still children. *And they were scared.*

These people were so busy protecting themselves and trying to figure out what everything meant, they didn't do what they most needed to do: relax, be who they were, and allow themselves to shine.

They didn't know it was okay to stop protecting themselves. They didn't know it was okay to love and be loved. They didn't know they could love themselves.

When I awoke, I realized I was one of them.

This book is dedicated to us, the recovering adult children and codependents. May we each awaken to the beauty of ourselves, other people, and life.

For helping make this book possible, I thank God, Nichole, Shane, Mom, John, Becky, Terry, Ruth, Scott, Lee, Linda, Carolyn, and my readers. Some encouraged and inspired me to write; some had to put up with me while I did.

Contents

Acknowledgments

First, I want to acknowledge the recovering people who shared their stories with me. They brought life to my work.

I also want to acknowledge the contributions of Timmen Cermak, M.D., a founding member and first president of the National Association for Children of Alcoholics, and Bedford Combs, M.Ed., LMFT, Founding President of the South Carolina Association for Children of Alcoholics. Their work helped me understand the recovery process, and they helped me grow.

"Have you been writing any personal experience articles lately?" the woman asked the writer. "No," replied the writer. "I've been busy having them."
— *Ruth Peterman*[1]

Introduction

This is a book about recovery.

Actually, this is a book about continuing our recoveries.

I wrote it for people recovering from the ways they've allowed themselves to be affected by other people and their problems. I wrote it for people recovering from codependency, chemical dependency, and adult children issues. I wrote it for people struggling to master the art of self-care.

Codependent No More, my last book, was about stopping the pain and gaining control of our lives. This book is about what to do when the pain has stopped and we've begun to suspect we have lives to live. It's about what happens next.

We'll look at recovery, relapse, doing our family of origin work, and what to do about it after we've done it. We'll talk about relationships. We'll talk about concepts like surrender and spirituality too.

We'll talk about many ideas: dealing with shame, growing in self-esteem, overcoming deprivation, sharing recovery with our children, and getting beyond our fatal attractions long enough to find relationships that work.

When I began this manuscript, I had a long list of scattered bits of information I wanted to parlay. I wasn't certain how these ideas would fit together. When I stopped trying to control, the book took on, as some do, a unique and occa-

---

Editor's note: An Endnotes section, which lists footnotes in each chapter, appears at the end of every chapter in this book.

sionally surprising life of its own.

Codependent No More was about beginning our recoveries. This book is about the core issues of recovery: working on the nuts and bolts, and fine-tuning.

In retrospect, it has emerged primarily as a book about growing in self-love, and our ability to affirm and nurture ourselves. A serendipity of that process is growing in our capacity to love others and to let them, and God, love us.

This book is based on research, my personal and professional experiences, and my opinion. Throughout, I'll attempt to attribute all ideas, theories, and quotes to appropriate sources. Sometimes it's difficult to do that in the recovery field because many people say many of the same things.

The case histories I use are true. I've changed names and details to protect people's privacy.

I've included activities at the end of some chapters. You can explore your answers in a separate journal or notebook.

Also, this book is not about how to change or help the other person. It's about knowing it's okay for us to continue helping ourselves, to better lives and improved relationships.

An old adage says, "When the student is ready, the teacher will appear." Another, however, says, "You teach what you most need to learn."

Writers, they say, are teachers.

"It is possible," wrote Lawrence Block, "to see everything we write as a letter to ourselves, designed to convey to one portion of ourselves the lesson that another portion has already learned."[2]

I have learned from writing this book. I hope you gain as much from reading it.

ENDNOTES

1. Ruth Peterman is a Minneapolis writer and writing teacher. She told this story during a class she taught.

2. Lawrence Block, "Messages for Your Most Important Reader," *Writer's Digest* (June 1988): 68.

SECTION I

RECOVERY

*Recovery is when
fun becomes fun;
love becomes love;
and life becomes worth living.*

I started taking care of myself and it feels so good
I'm not going to stop, no matter what.
— *Anonymous*

The Recovery Movement

Something exciting is happening across the land. Let's take a look.

Carla's Story

Two years ago, Carla thought she was crazy and her schedule was normal.

"Well, almost normal," said Carla, an elementary school teacher and the thirty-five-year-old daughter of a well-groomed, professional family.

From 6 to 8 A.M., Carla worked at a day-care center. From 8:30 A.M. to 12:30 P.M., she taught grade school. From 2 to 6 P.M., she taught at an after-school latchkey program.

To save a woman from being sent to a nursing home, Carla had moved in with an Alzheimer's victim. So at 12:30, Carla rushed home to make lunch for her roommate. At supper time, Carla rushed home again to make supper for her roommate.

Several years earlier, while working at the state prison, Carla had befriended, then fallen in love with, an inmate (a phenomenon peculiar to many people who identify with codependency). After washing the supper dishes, Carla hurried to the prison to visit him. At 9 P.M., Carla dashed home to put her roommate to bed.

In her spare time, Carla volunteered forty hours each month

to the county mental health center. And she taught Sunday school.

Besides those volunteer activities, Carla had offered use of her home, rent-free, to a family she met at the prison visiting room. She was able to do this because she had left her home standing empty when she moved in with the Alzheimer's patient.

"I thought I was doing everything right. I was doing everything people expected of me. I was being good to people. I was being a good Christian. One thing I couldn't understand was why everyone was mad at me," Carla says. "The other thing I couldn't understand was why I felt crazy and wished I was dead.

"The relatives of the woman I lived with got angry at me for telling them how sick she was and how much care she needed. My boyfriend was mad at me. My bosses were upset because I kept getting sick and missing work. And the woman living in my house got angry because when she began working, I started asking for rent money.

"I didn't know how I felt," Carla says. "For as long as I can remember, I couldn't remember feeling joy, sorrow, anything! I knew I was physically sick. My legs and feet were swollen so badly I couldn't walk some days. But I didn't go to the doctor because I didn't want to bother him.

"I didn't want to bother the doctor," she says, shaking her head. "Things were crazy, but they were about to get crazier."

The woman living in Carla's house became so indignant about paying rent she moved out. Carla moved back into her home. Within days, the furnace went out, the sewer pipe collapsed, the basement flooded, and gophers chewed through the gas line and the house almost blew up. A neighbor selling his property used the wrong land description and instead sold Carla's house, and a pheasant flew through the bay window, decapitated itself, and ran through the house like a dead chicken.

"Just like me," Carla recalls.

Soon, Carla's boyfriend, an alcoholic, was released from prison. Within two weeks he started drinking and disappeared from her life.

"I bottomed out. This was the culmination of over thirty years of failure," Carla says. "I felt like a failure professionally and personally. I had gone from one hundred fifteen pounds to over two hundred pounds. I had been married and divorced twice, both times to successful professional men who physically or verbally abused me. Now, I had been rejected by a prison inmate. This was it. This was the end! I hadn't drank for fifteen years, but I started drinking two quarts of vodka a day. I wanted to die."

Carla didn't die. Instead, someone handed her a book about codependency. From reading it, she learned that although her behaviors were a little crazy, she wasn't. She was battling codependency. She also learned a recovery program was available to her, one that promised to change her life.

Although she's worked at recovery for only a year and a half, Carla has worked hard at it. She regularly attends both Al-Anon and Alcoholics Anonymous meetings. She goes to workshops on codependency, shame, and self-esteem. She also works with a therapist experienced with codependency recovery issues.

"I got mad at the therapist," Carla recalls. "I was a professional; he was a professional. I went to him expecting him to do his job: fix me. He told me he couldn't do that. I learned there wasn't a magic cure. I learned I had to do my own recovery work."

Although she didn't find a magic cure, Carla describes the changes in her life in eighteen months as "dramatic."

"I've done a lot of grieving, but at least I'm feeling. I'm feeling feelings for the first time in my life. I'm feeling sad, and I'm feeling happy.

"I'm still busy, but I'm not running around like a chicken with its head chopped off. I'm choosing to do the things I'm doing, instead of feeling like I have no choices. I'm setting and reaching goals. That feels good," Carla says.

Carla is still struggling to undo the financial chaos connected to her codependency. "But at least I'm struggling for and toward something. I now have money in my checkbook. I can take myself out to eat. And I've even started buying myself new clothes. That's different. I used to shop at secondhand stores and deliberately chose the worst items there, the things I thought nobody else would want. I didn't want to take any clothing away from the poor people," she explains, "the ones who really needed it."

Carla has made other advances too. She's learning to say no. She's learning to stick up for herself and her rights, instead of fighting only for the rights of others. She's beginning to look back to discover the origins of her codependency (family of origin work).

"My family wasn't bad or awful," Carla says. "They were good, smart, professional people. Although my father abused prescription drugs for about two years, my parents weren't obviously addicted or dysfunctional. They were close. We had some fun times.

"But there were subtleties," Carla adds. "I learned how to be a martyr. I always felt I needed to be perfect. I never felt good enough. I didn't know how to deal with feelings. We lived in a small community. During one phase of my childhood, my parents' political stance caused us to be ostracized by the town. I felt so rejected. And I learned how to reject *myself*. I started believing something was wrong with me."

Besides looking back, Carla has begun to look around. She's noticing how codependency has permeated her life.

"I have two groups of friends: other codependents who want to complain about being victims, and the people who want to use and mistreat me. I'm working at changing my friendships. I'm also reevaluating my professional life. My codependency influenced my career choices. Most of my jobs demanded a lot and gave me little in return. Of course, I gave and gave on my jobs, then got angry because I felt used. Now,

I'm learning to set boundaries at work. Some people are getting mad at me for changing, but I'm not feeling so used.

"I'm learning to stop asking why people are doing this to me," Carla says. "I've started asking why I'm allowing them to do this to me."

Relationships with men are still a weak spot in Carla's recovery. "I'm still attracted to the sickest man in the room, the one who needs me the most," Carla admits. "But at least I've started to get red flags. That's new. I always used to get green lights."

She says she has much work left to do on self-esteem but has begun to accept herself. "I do a lot of work with affirmations. I've got my bathroom mirror pasted full of them. That helps. It really does.

"Sometimes I still let other people control me. Sometimes I'm not sure when it's okay to want approval from people, and when it's a codependent behavior. I'm not always sure when it's okay to give, and when I'm doing caretaking stuff. And sometimes I get scared.

"But the best thing that's happened to me is I've begun to feel peaceful," Carla says. "For the first time in my life I want to live, and I believe there's a purpose for my life.

"My relationship with my Higher Power, God, has improved. I'm not in control of my life, but by working my program, it's become manageable. I know Someone is caring for me and helping me care for myself.

"And," Carla adds, "I'm proud of my recovery."

Recently, while paging through a photo album, Carla found one of the few pictures taken of her when she was a child. She rarely allowed people to photograph her because she hated the way she looked.

"I was surprised when I saw this picture," Carla says. "I wasn't ugly. There wasn't anything so terribly wrong with me, like I thought there was. It's sad I've spent so many years of my life believing there was."

The other day, when Carla walked into the student bathroom at the grade school where she works, she found a sobbing fourth-grade girl curled up behind the trash can. The girl, a beautiful child with long dark hair, had tried to smash the bathroom mirror.

Carla asked what was wrong. The girl said she hated herself, she hated the way she looked, and she wanted to die. Carla gently scooped up the child, carried her into the office, and referred her to the school psychiatrist.

"I cried for her, and I cried for me. But it wasn't all tears of sadness," Carla says. "I cried because I felt relieved. At last we have hope."

Our Stories

That's the good news, and that's what this book is about: hope for Carla, hope for the little girl who hates herself, hope for you, and hope for me. This book is about hope for continued recovery from this problem we've come to call codependency.

Many of us have found that hope. By the numbers, we're flocking to Twelve Step meetings, workshops, and therapists — to get help for ourselves. We're demanding (well, "inquiring about," at least initially) our birthright, our right to be, our right to live, and our right to recover.

Celebrities are publicly declaring themselves adult children of alcoholics. Men, women, and young children (not just adult children) are beginning their searches for hope. I've heard from older people who have just begun their recoveries. "I'm seventy-five years old and I feel like I'm just learning to live," said one woman. "But at least I'm learning."

Codependent jokes have emerged. Did you hear about the codependent wife? Each morning, she wakes her husband and asks him how she's going to feel that day.

Codependency even made the pages of *Newsweek* magazine.[1]

The important idea here is we've lost our invisibility. We're recognizing ourselves, and others are recognizing us too.

More help and hope has become available to us — from teddy bears that tell us it's okay to feel what we feel, to in-patient codependency treatment programs where we can deal with our inner child (the part of us that feels, plays, and needs to be nurtured) and where we can address our family of origin issues (our messages from the past that control what we do today — like a computer program). And we're taking advantage of it.

We're part of a groundswell movement, a tremendous movement that's come into its own time. We're saying, simply and clearly, enough is enough, and we've suffered enough. It's time to do things differently.

For years, we called chemical dependency and other disorders "family diseases." Now, we're believing our own words. At last, as Carla said, we have hope. Practical hope. The word *codependency* may label a problem, but to many of us it also labels the solution: recovery.

Many of us have suffered, and are still suffering to some degree, from a relationship with a dysfunctional person. Sometimes that person appeared in our childhoods, sometimes in our adult lives. Usually, we've had relationships with more than one dysfunctional person; this pattern began in childhood and repeated itself as we grew older.

Discovering that many of us have suffered to some extent from codependency has affirmed one of my earlier beliefs: it's okay to be codependent. It has to be; there are so many of us. But it's even better to be recovering.

Some of us have been recovering for a long time; others are just beginning the recovery experience. Some of us are working on dual or multiple recovery programs; for instance, recovery from codependency and chemical dependency, or recovery from codependency and an eating disorder. We may not always be certain what it means to be recovering or where our recovery programs will take us, but we're going there anyway.

We may be codependent "not as much" while we're striving to be codependent no more, but we're getting better all the time. And that's good enough.

What does the future hold?

The word *codependency* may disappear. Media and public attention may subside. But no matter what we call it, recovery from codependency is more than a fad. We've started the journey of self-care and self-love. Although there may be a few detours and resting places along the way, we're not going to stop now.

Let me wrap up this chapter with an anecdote about my son, Shane, who loves video games. Recently, he got involved playing a particular game. This game offered about forty levels of skill, each deeper and more complicated than the last, to those who could overcome the obstacles, avoid the pitfalls, stay empowered by the power source, and not get killed by the enemy.

Shane was playing well enough, but couldn't get past a certain level of play. No matter how hard he tried, he couldn't go any further. After a while, he stopped believing it was possible to go further.

. Then one day a friend stopped by, and my son watched her play the game. She'd been playing longer; she'd watched an older brother play; she'd learned a few tricks. She could jump, hop, and scurry her way down to the deepest levels.

Watching her was all it took. After that, with confidence and ease, my son began to play at increasingly deeper levels. He got unstuck. He broke through.

That's what this book is about: believing we can go further than we've ever gone before. Let's love ourselves for how far we've come. Let's see how far we can go. And let's go there together. We each have to do our own work, but doing it together is what makes it work.

ENDNOTES

1. Charles Leerhsen, with Tessa Namuth, "Alcohol and the Family," *Newsweek* (18 January 1988).

CHAPTER 2

*What's a codependent? The answer's easy. They're
some of the most loving, caring people I know.*
                                    — *Lonny Owen*[1]

Recovery

In spite of the emergence of the word *codependency*, and so
many people recovering from it, it is still jargon. No standard
definition exists. We haven't agreed on whether
codependency is a sickness, a condition, or a normal response
to abnormal people. We still haven't agreed on whether it's
hyphenated: *codependency* or *co-dependency*?

What most people have decided is this: whatever
codependency is, it's a problem, and recovering from it feels
better than not.

If codependency is so common, why bother to call it anything? Why not just call it normal? Because it hurts. And
recovery means learning how to stop the pain. In this chapter,
we'll explore what it means to do that.

To explain recovery, let me indulge in a metaphor. In 1982,
a fire nearly destroyed my home. I learned some truths then
about fires.

The fire's not over when the fire truck leaves. Repairing fire
damage can involve an extensive, sometimes frustrating rehabilitation process.

A fire can smolder for a long time before it bursts into flames. The
fire in my home smoldered quietly, but dangerously, in a
mattress for hours before it became apparent. I had been in
the room minutes before flames erupted, and the room looked
"fine."

*Although we physically survive a fire, we can be affected —
traumatized — mentally and emotionally.* For years after my fire,
each time I saw a fire truck speeding to a fire, each time I heard
sirens, or saw a burning house on the news, I panicked. My
chest tightened. My breath quickened. My hands trembled.
When leaving home, I checked and double checked to make
certain no hazards existed. *I no longer felt safe.*

These same truths apply to another fire, the one we've
come to label codependency. It can require an extensive,
sometimes frustrating rehabilitation process. It can smolder
for a long time before it bursts into flames. And, though we've
survived the fire, many of us have been traumatized.

Let's explore these ideas.

The Fire's Not Out When the Fire Truck Leaves

Many good definitions of codependency have surfaced.

In 1987, a handout at a week-long training seminar on
chemical dependency and the family, sponsored by the
Johnson Institute of Minneapolis, described codependency as
"a set of maladaptive, compulsive behaviors learned by family members to survive in a family experiencing great emotional pain and stress. . . . Behaviors . . . passed on from
generation to generation whether alcoholism is present or
not."

Earnie Larsen, the recovery pioneer from Minnesota, calls
codependency "those self-defeating learned behaviors or
character defects that result in a diminished capacity to initiate, or participate in, loving relationships."

A friend, and recovering woman, defines codependents as
"people who don't take care of themselves, whether or not
they are, or have ever been, in a relationship with an alcoholic."

And in *Codependent No More* I called a codependent "a
person who has let someone else's behavior affect him or her,
and is obsessed with controlling other people's behavior."

These definitions refer to behaviors — today's self-defeating, learned survival behaviors. Certainly, recovery means extinguishing any fires blazing in our homes and lives today. But the heart of recovery is the sometimes grueling, extensive reconstruction process of acquiring new behaviors. In recovery, we stop enduring life and begin to live it.

Instead of obsessively trying to control others, we learn to detach. Instead of allowing others to hurt and use us, we set boundaries. Instead of reacting, we learn to relax and let things settle into place. We replace tunnel vision with perspective. We forego worrying and denial, and learn constructive problem solving skills. We learn to feel and express feelings; we learn to value what we want and need; we stop punishing ourselves for other people's problems, nonsense, and insanity. We stop expecting ourselves to be perfect, and we stop expecting perfection of others.

We stop reacting to the powerfully dysfunctional systems so many of us have been affected by. We stop getting tangled up in craziness. We acquire the art of removing ourselves as victims.

We stop compulsively taking care of other people and we take care of ourselves. We learn to be good to ourselves, to have fun, and to enjoy life. We learn to feel good about what we've accomplished. We stop focusing on what's wrong and we notice what's right. We learn to function in relationships. We learn to love ourselves, so we can better love others.

Recovery also means addressing any other issues or compulsive behaviors that have cropped up along the way. Codependency is sneaky and deceptive. It's also progressive. One thing leads to another, and often things get worse.

We may become workaholics, or busy freaks. We may develop eating disorders or abuse mood-altering chemicals. We may develop compulsive sexual behaviors or become compulsive about spending, religion, achievement, or appearance.

Other complications can emerge too. We can become chronically depressed, develop emotional or mental problems, or stress-related illnesses.

"We hear a lot about how alcoholism is terminal for the alcoholic," says one recovering man. "We don't hear enough about how codependency can be terminal too. So many of us wind up thinking about, or trying to, kill ourselves."

Recovery means dealing with the entire package of self-defeating, compulsive behaviors, and any other problems that may have emerged. But we don't deal with these behaviors or problems by thinking we're bad for having them. We address ourselves, and recovery, with a sense of forgiveness and a certain gentleness toward ourselves. We begin to understand that the behaviors we've used were survival tools. We've been coping. We've been doing the best we could. We've been protecting ourselves. Some recovery professionals suggest these behaviors may have saved our lives.

"If we hadn't protected ourselves, we may have given up or developed a fatal illness and died," says Bedford Combs.[2]

Whether it's a compulsion to caretake, control, work, or eat pecan pies, compulsive behaviors initially are about stopping the pain.[3] We begin to realize what we've been doing: trying to stop the pain. But we begin to understand something else too. Although compulsive behaviors may help us temporarily avoid feelings or problems, they don't really stop the pain. They create more. They may even take on a habitual and problematic life of their own.

So we acquire new behaviors, gradually, sometimes with reluctance, and usually with a great deal of experimentation and forward and backward movement.

We don't change perfectly or completely. Sometimes, in recovery, we still protect ourselves with survival behaviors. Sometimes we need to do that. Sometimes we regress, and that's okay too. Sometimes, we turn our behaviors around and let them work for us, instead of against us. For instance, in recovery, many of us have used our ability to endure deprivation to *help ourselves* get through college.

In recovery, we still give to people. We continue to care about people. But we learn we are responsible for our behaviors, and our behaviors have consequences. We learn some behaviors have self-defeating consequences, while others have beneficial consequences. We learn we have choices.

We also learn we don't change by ourselves, or by exerting greater amounts of willpower. Intertwined with this process of changing our behaviors is a Higher Power, God, as we each understand Him. Paradoxically, we change most during those tremendous moments when we run out of willpower.

Recovery means acquiring, living by, and sometimes living and recovering *because of* spiritual principles. We learn to do intangible things like "Let Go and Let God," "surrender," and "accept" while we're doing the more tangible behaviors such as making decisions and setting boundaries.

Changing today's self-defeating behaviors is an important part of recovery. It's where most of us begin. It's what most of us need to work on for the duration. But recovery is more than that.

The Smoldering Coals

When I first began my recovery from codependency, I assumed my codependency started when I formed relationships with the alcoholics in my life. I now believe my codependency was the reason I had so many alcoholics in my life.

A fire had been smoldering for many years in me, probably since I was a child. That fire burst into flames in my thirties, when I bottomed out and wanted to end my life.

Some of the smoldering coals in that fire were the rules, *the codependent rules.*

Robert Subby, a codependency and adult children recovery professional, talks about codependency being "an emotional, psychological, and behavioral condition that develops as a result of an individual's prolonged exposure to, and practice of, a set of oppressive rules."[4]

These rules say:

- Don't feel or talk about feelings.
- Don't think.
- Don't identify, talk about, or solve problems.
- Don't be who you are — be good, right, strong, and perfect.
- Don't be selfish — take care of others and neglect yourself.
- Don't have fun, don't be silly or enjoy life.
- Don't trust other people or yourself.
- Don't be vulnerable.
- Don't be direct.
- Don't get close to people.
- Don't grow, change, or in any way rock this family's boat.[5]

These rules probably weren't pasted on the refrigerator next to "clean up your room" and "take out the garbage," but they might as well have been.

More coals in that fire were the *other messages* I interpreted while growing up. These messages included beliefs such as:

- I'm not lovable.
- I don't deserve good things.
- I'll never succeed.

And for many of us, the smoldering fire contains other coals too. Included among these are *feelings from our childhood*, feelings that hurt too much to feel. Many of us denied these feelings, then lived out situations that recreated the same feelings we were denying from our childhoods. The smoldering fire is a past buried alive, according to Earnie Larsen.

"I always knew my dad was an alcoholic," says a recovering woman. "It wasn't until recently I realized I was an adult child of an alcoholic. It wasn't until recently I realized how I felt about him being an alcoholic. It wasn't until recently I realized how much I had been affected by the disease."

Codependency is about the ways we have been affected by other people and our pasts.

Some of us grew up in powerfully dysfunctional family systems. Some of us lived in those systems as children, then recreated the experience as adults. We may have spent much of our lifetimes being affected by, and reacting to, systems too powerful to budge.

We may have spent lifetimes wondering what was wrong with us when the other person, or the system, was "what was wrong." Many of us have surpassed being "affected." Many of us have been, to some degree, traumatized.[6]

In his writings about codependency and the adult child syndrome, Timmen Cermak calls this "Post Traumatic Stress Disorder." According to Cermak, it can happen to people who chronically live through or with events "outside the range of what is considered to be normal human experience."[7]

The symptoms of stress disorder in codependency are similar to the symptoms of stress disorder in war veterans. The symptoms are comparable to the way I was affected by the fire that burned my home.

We may, without warning, reexperience the feelings, thoughts, and behaviors that were present during the original traumatic event.[8] Codependent feelings and behaviors — fear, anxiety, shame, an overwhelming need to control, neglecting ourselves, and focusing on others — may suddenly emerge when something in our environment, something innocuous, reminds us or our subconscious of something noxious that happened before.

These reactions may have been entirely appropriate when we went through the original experience, but these reactions may be inappropriate, confusing, and self-defeating today.

After the fire, events that triggered a stress reaction in me were: hearing sirens, seeing fire trucks speeding by, watching a home burn on the news. After living with an alcoholic, or living through another kind of trauma, many events can be "triggers."

"For children from chemically dependent families, the trigger can be almost anything," Cermak writes, "the sound of ice clinking in a glass, an expression of anger or criticism, arguing, the sensation of losing control. . . ."[9]

Another symptom of stress disorder is *psychic numbing*. Cermak describes this as suspending feelings in favor of taking steps to ensure our safety, or splitting between one's self and one's experience.[10] To protect ourselves, to keep things going, to keep ourselves going, we disconnect from our feelings — our *selves*. We go into "freeze" or "survival" mode.

Still another symptom of stress disorder is *hypervigilance*, an inability to feel comfortable unless we're continually monitoring our surroundings. "They remained on edge," Cermak writes, "always expecting the worst, unable to trust or feel safe again."[11]

Cermak is describing Vietnam veterans, but his statement applies to many of us. We stay on guard. We watch, listen, and worry, wondering when the other shoe will drop. We no longer feel safe.

Finally, in discussing this syndrome, Cermak talks about survivor guilt. "Whenever they begin to experience the fullness that life has to offer, they immediately feel as if they are betraying those who never had the chance." He's describing people who survived a war that others didn't. "It seems somehow wrong to go away and be healthy when those who are left behind are still suffering."[12]

Recovery means changing today's self-defeating, learned survival behaviors. Recovery means putting out the smoldering coals. And recovery means dealing with any ways we may have been traumatized.

We reconnect with ourselves. We learn to give ourselves some love and concern. We learn to make ourselves feel safe. We know, really know, it's okay for us to be as healthy as we can become.

We're not crazy. We're codependent. And recovery means putting out the fire.

In the next chapter, we'll look at how that happens.

ENDNOTES

1. Lonny Owen, C.A.C. Facilitator, has been working in the codependency field for eight years as of the writing of this book. He and I facilitated a ten-week workshop/support group for codependents in Minneapolis in 1988.

2. This statement came from Bedford Combs, M.Ed., LMFT, at a workshop he presented entitled, "Moving Through Unfinished Business: The Recovery Journey from Codependency." The workshop took place on 25 March 1988, in Charlotte, North Carolina. Combs is founding president of the South Carolina Association for Children of Alcoholics, Director of CHAPS Family Care in South Carolina, and is a clinical member of AAMFT.

3. This thought has been around recovery circles for years, but I derived it specifically for content here from Combs' workshop (footnote 2).

4. Robert Subby, "Inside the Chemically Dependent Marriage: Denial & Manipulation," quoted in *Co-Dependency, An Emerging Issue* (Hollywood, Fla.: Health Communications, Inc., 1984), 26.

5. Robert Subby, and John Friel, "Co-Dependency — A Paradoxical Dependency," quoted in *Co-Dependency, An Emerging Issue* (Hollywood, Fla.: Health Communications, Inc., 1984), 31-44.

6. My writing on codependency and Post Traumatic Stress Disorder is based on writings by Timmen L. Cermak, M.D. Cermak is a founding board member, president, and chair of the National Association for Children of Alcoholics and co-director of Genesis, a San Francisco-based treatment and consultation program for the family aspects of chemical dependency.

7. Timmen L. Cermak, *Diagnosing and Treating Co-Dependence* (Minneapolis: Johnson Institute, 1986), 55.

8. Ibid.

9. Ibid.
10. Ibid., 56.
11. Ibid., 57.
12. Ibid., 57-58.

CHAPTER 3

*I can tell you what it was like, and I can tell you
what it's like now but I'm still not sure what
happened.*

— *Anonymous*

The Process

Recovery is a process. Recovery is a process. How many times have we heard that? We've heard it so many times because it's true. Recovery is a process, a gradual one of awareness, acceptance, and change. It's also a healing process. Yet, recovery often feels more like "being processed."

Both ideas are true. Recovery is a process by which we change, and by which we become changed. The important ideas here are learning when it's time to do something, and when it's time to let something happen.

Although our recovery experiences are unique, there are similarities. Timmen Cermak and other professionals have identified certain recovery stages.[1] In this chapter, we'll explore those stages which are:

- survival/denial
- reidentification
- core issues
- reintegration
- genesis

Survival/Denial

In this pre-recovery stage, denial operates unbidden (borrowing a line from Robin Norwood)[2], and we're using our coping behaviors to survive. We don't see things too painful to see; we don't feel emotions too painful to feel. We don't realize our coping behaviors are self-defeating. In fact, we're often proud of our gestures.

"Look at all the people I'm taking care of," we tell people. "See what I did to control him!" We may take pride in our ability to deprive ourselves or stifle feelings.

"It's not that bad," we tell others and ourselves. "Things will be better tomorrow." "I'll get my reward in heaven." Or,"Everything's fine. Baby's back in my arms again!" We may smile and say, "Things are fine," but things aren't fine.[3] We've lost touch with ourselves. We're existing, not living.

Then something happens. Maybe it's one big problem. Maybe it's several smaller problems, or many large ones. Maybe it's the same problem that's happened so many times before. What changes is our reaction. We become fed up. We run out of willpower. We run out of ourselves.

We realize, on some level, that our lives have become unmanageable. Regardless of what the other person is or isn't doing, we know our lives aren't working. We've been enduring life, not living it. And we become ready to be changed. Although we may not be sure *what*, we know *something* has to change. Something does. We move on to the next stage.

Reidentification

Two important events take place here.

We reidentify ourselves and our behaviors. I become Melody, a recovering codependent (or adult child or Al-Anon). Instead of taking pride in our coping behaviors, we begin to see them as self-defeating.

And we surrender. We wave the white flag. We accept our powerlessness over other people, their problems, our pasts, our messages from the past, our circumstances, sometimes ourselves and our feelings, or any other appropriate area. We begin to establish, as Timmen Cermak puts it, "a realistic relationship with willpower."[4]

Some people, like Carla from the first chapter, feel immensely relieved upon getting to this point in the journey. "I was so glad to find out I wasn't crazy; I was codependent," she says.

Others feel angry. "I was furious when I discovered I had a problem with codependency," recalls one man. "I was mad at God, mad at life, and mad because I had to wait until I was fifty-five years old to find out why my life wasn't working."

Besides feeling angry or relieved, we start feeling many of the feelings we've been freezing. We thaw out. We do this when we feel safe enough to do this. We begin to feel all the sadness and pain we've been working so hard to avoid. We begin our grief work. Some of us have more loss to face than others.

"My recovery began when I left my home and my sex addict husband, in an ambulance headed for a psychiatric ward," says Sheryl. "I wanted to commit suicide, but I didn't. I wanted to leave my husband, but I couldn't bring myself to do that either. I asked God to get me out if He wanted me out, and my answer came the day the ambulance took me away. I was released from the hospital six weeks later, but I never went back to my husband.

"For the first year, I cried every day for hours," Sheryl recalls. "I faced the financial chaos created by my destructive relationship. I had borrowed and borrowed to live a lifestyle we couldn't afford. I was barely able to work. I had to take a job under my usual level. I felt suicidal, and the emotional pain was overwhelming. I took antidepressants, went to support groups four nights a week, and almost lived at the psychiatrist's office. I was scared, hopeless, and shaken to the bone. I felt," Sheryl says, "like a wounded deer.

"Things are better now. I still miss my ex-husband from time to time, but I don't want him back. I'm still struggling financially, but I've paid off some bills. I've taken a better job, and I'm living in a nicer apartment. In fact, I'm living. I've got my brains and my life out of hock and no matter where I go, I intend to take them with me. It's been a long haul and I don't ever want to go back. I'm not willing to. And the good thing is, I don't have to."

Some recovering people seek professional help during this stage. Some go on antidepressant therapy for a time. And, like Sheryl, some take jobs beneath their usual level of competence. This can be necessary, but frustrating.

"I'm a dentist. My boyfriend is an alcoholic and a womanizer," explains another woman. "He left me. Now he's living with another woman. He's working. I'm so depressed I can't work. I lay on my couch eating chocolates and turning into the great white whale. I'm so mad. He can go on with his life, and mine has stopped. It's not fair."

This stage of recovery can be confusing. We're just recouping from hitting our lowest point. Our grief work may take much of our energy. And, though we've begun recovering, we haven't yet acquired new living tools.

Now is when we begin experimenting with recovery concepts like detachment, not reacting as much, and letting go. It is a time for diligent evaluation of those things we cannot control. It is a time for acceptance. In this stage, we begin connecting with other people who are recovering. In this stage, we establish, or reestablish, our relationship with a Higher Power. We begin connecting, or reconnecting, with ourselves.

This is a time to remember that we are more than our pain and more than our problems. It's a time to cling to hope. The healing process has begun. Like healing from a physical condition, it hurts most the day after surgery.

Core Issues

This stage can be fun, occasionally overwhelming, but fun.

Here, the lights come on. We see and understand more about ourselves and our behaviors. We become aware. And aware. And aware . . . Often, we feel uncertain about what to do with all this awareness.

We look back and see how long we've been using our

self-defeating behaviors. We look around and see how codependency has permeated our lives. But, we're looking and moving forward too.

We begin setting goals. We begin experimenting with new behaviors. We get better at detachment. We learn different ways of caring for and nurturing ourselves. We begin setting boundaries. We get better at dealing with feelings, including anger. We may tenuously take first steps toward learning how to have fun. We start practicing new relationship and living skills. We may try something new, get scared, and go back to our old ways for a while. We may end relationships, get scared, then go back to check those out for a time too.

We may stay stuck in a state of awareness — knowing we're doing a particular thing, but feeling unable to do much about it.

Within a short time span, we may feel scared, excited, hopeless, and hopeful. Some days, we wonder if anything is happening. Other days, we're certain too much is happening. Some days, we wake knowing all, indeed, is well.

In this stage, recovery begins to have less to do with coping with "the other person." It becomes more of a personal affair — a private journey of finding and building a "self" and a life. We may start to dream and hope again, but our hopes usually center on our own dreams, not someone else's. We may get protective of the new life and self we're building.

Throughout, we're working a program. We're going to our meetings, working with a therapist (if that's appropriate), and connecting with healthy, supportive friends.

This is a time of experimentation and growth. It's a time of becoming more comfortable with new behaviors, and less comfortable with old ones. Our newly-formed beliefs about what we can and cannot change grow stronger. It's a time when we start to figure out what it means to take care of ourselves. We try, fail, try, succeed, try some more, fail some more, and through it all, make a little progress.

It's a time to be patient.

Reintegration

Since we started this journey, we've been struggling with power issues: powerlessness and finding a Higher Power. Now comes the exciting and paradoxical part of this journey. Through powerlessness and surrender we find our personal power. We become empowered to do the possible — live our own lives. Owning our power is as important as learning to accept powerlessness.

In this stage, we discover ourselves as complete, healthy, imperfect but lovable and certainly adequate. We become comfortable with ourselves. We come back home to live with ourselves.

We learn to respect and love ourselves. We find ourselves loving others too, and allowing them to love us in healthy ways that feel good. We accept the fact that we're good enough.

We are neither running around spewing feelings, nor are we repressing them. We're feeling feelings and knowing that's okay. We make mistakes but we know that's okay, and we try to learn from them as best we can. Although a tendency to control may still be our instinctive response to situations, detachment becomes a secondary reaction — for by now, we're certain we can't control others.

Sometimes, we slip into caretaking, shame, and martyrdom. But we get out. We may still feel guilty when we say no, set a boundary, or refuse to take care of someone, but we know the guilt will pass. We've gained the confidence that taking care of ourselves is in everyone's best interests. We've learned we can take care of ourselves. And what we can't do, God can and will do for us.

By this time, we've accepted the premise that problems are an ongoing part of life. We don't dwell on this, but we've gained a degree of confidence in our problem-solving skills. Our messages from the past haven't disappeared, but we develop a keener ear for identifying when these messages are trying to sabotage us.

Our relationships with ourselves, our friends, our family, and our Higher Power have improved. Intimacy becomes a reality.

We have become more comfortable with applying the four recovery power concepts: accepting powerlessness, finding a Higher Power, owning our personal power, and learning to share the power by participating in relationships.

We still feel frightened sometimes. We still have gray days. But they're gray, not black. And we know they'll pass.

When we reach this stage, life becomes more than something to be endured. At times, it's still tough. But sometimes it's downright peaceful and other times it's an adventure. And we're living it, all of it.

"I'm learning anything can happen," says one woman. "And 'anything' doesn't necessarily mean 'something bad' anymore."

Fun becomes fun; love becomes love; life becomes worth living. And we become grateful.

"Eight years ago, I went to a treatment center to get help for my alcoholic husband. Instead of helping my husband, the counselor told me to start helping myself," says Lisa.

Lisa started working on her recovery, and she worked hard at it. She went to her Al-Anon meetings. She put herself through college. She learned how to take care of herself.

"When I went to that counselor eight years ago, I was a mess. Living through my husband's alcoholism was the worst thing that ever happened to me. But it was also the best," Lisa says. "If it hadn't been so bad, I wouldn't have gotten off dead center and found a life for myself. And for that, I'm grateful."

During this stage of recovery, we continue our involvement with Twelve Step programs. We still need to ask for help sometimes, and we still need understanding and acceptance. But the healing process is well under way.

Genesis

This isn't the end. It's a new beginning. We're no longer carrying around "imprisoned" selves. Nor are we indulging in all our whims and desires. Discipline has found its place in our lives too. Like butterflies broken loose from a cocoon, our selves are "flying free," yet surrendered to a loving, caring Higher Power. We've found a new way of life — one that works.

This is the recovery process. It's a fluid process, with carry-overs and crossovers to the different stages. There isn't a fixed time frame for moving through these stages.

It begins through the grace of God. It continues in the same manner, assisted by our commitment to the process. Recovery is many things. It's a gradual process, a healing process, and a predictable process. But it's also a spiritual process.

What's our part?

- Attending Twelve Step meetings or other appropriate support groups.
- Applying the Steps and other recovery concepts in our lives.
- Working with a therapist, if appropriate.
- Attending seminars and workshops.
- Maintaining an attitude of honesty, openness, and willingness to try.
- Struggling through the frustration, awkwardness, and discomfort of change.
- Connecting with other recovering people.
- Reading meditation books and other helpful literature.
- Continuing to surrender.

Our part means having the courage to feel what we need to feel, and do what we need to do. Our part is doing our own recovery work. If we cooperate, to the best of our ability, with this process, we'll know what to do and when to do that.

Recovery isn't something we do perfectly or at once. Neither concept applies here.

"I'm still real controlling, but at least I recognize when I'm doing it," says one woman.

"I'm going right home and ask for what I want and need," says another, "just as soon as I figure out what that is."

These comments represent recovery as much as any tremendous "before and after" tale. Struggling is okay. Backstepping is okay. Small bits of progress are not only okay, they're admirable.

People who have been recovering for a while may become more comfortable dealing with certain situations because they've encountered similar situations so many times before, but they still struggle.

Some days, my feelings flow freely through me. Self-acceptance comes naturally, as though it has always been my friend. I don't even feel shame about feeling ashamed. I simply acknowledge it, then move harmoniously into the next circumstance. I am part and parcel of the universe; there is a place for me, and I find delight, peace, and intimacy in that place. My life has been planned by a Loving Friend, and all I need do is show up.

Other days, I can't tell a feeling from a manhole cover. As one friend says, "I'm certain God has forgotten where I live."

Anne Morrow Lindbergh, in *Gift from the Sea*, writes:

> Vague as this definition may be, I believe most people are aware of periods in their lives when they seem to be "in grace" and other periods when they feel "out of grace," even though they may use different words to describe these states. "In the first happy condition, one seems to carry all one's tasks before one lightly, as if borne along on a great tide; and in the opposite state one can hardly tie a shoestring. It is true that a large part of life consists in learning a technique of tying the shoestring, whether one is in grace or not.

But there are techniques of living too; there are even techniques in the search for grace. And techniques can be cultivated.[5]

Much of recovery means learning to tie our shoestrings, whether we feel in grace or not, while we're cultivating recovery techniques. Some days go better than others.

A man approached me at a workshop one day. "I'm thirty-eight years old, and I've been recovering for three years," he said. "I'm dropping all the behaviors and coping mechanisms that have gotten me through this far in my life. I want so badly for the second half of my life to be as good as the first half has been miserable. The pain has stopped, but now I'm scared."

Well, I get scared too. I want the second half of my life to be as good as the first half was miserable. I get scared it won't be, and sometimes I get scared it will be. Sometimes, I'm just frightened. But I keep working at recovery anyway. I believe if we really want our lives to be different and better, and if we work toward that, our lives will be different and better.

Codependency is a progressive process, one of reaction, inaction, and malefaction.[6] One thing leads to another and things get worse. Recovery is also a progressive process — of action. If we take certain steps, we get better and so do things. Codependency takes on a life of its own, but so does recovery.

Recovery is a process, and we can trust that process. In spite of its ups and downs, back and forths, and blind spots, it works.

We can do our part, then let go and let ourselves grow.

Activity

1. What stage of the recovery process are you in?

2. What steps have you taken to do your part in the recovery process? Do you have a self-care plan? Do you go to Twelve Step meetings or other support groups? How often? Do you read a meditation book regularly? Are you seeing a therapist, or are you involved with another kind of therapy group? Do

you go to seminars or workshops? Do you read recovery books? Do you spend time with other recovering people?

3. If you've been recovering for a while, what are some of the things you did early in your recovery that helped you feel good? Are you still doing these things?[7]

4. What is the most recent action you've taken to do your part in your recovery? What did you gain from that?

ENDNOTES

1. Timmen L. Cermak, *Diagnosing and Treating Co-Dependence*, (Minneapolis, Johnson Institute, 1986), 68-93. The stages (names and information) are based on this book and Cermak's *A Time to Heal*. (Los Angeles: Jeremy P. Tarcher, Inc., 1988).

2. Robin Norwood, *Women Who Love Too Much*, (New York: Pocket Books, 1986), 140.

3. Scott Egleston. Mr. Egleston who is a private therapist and lives in the Twin Cities.

4. Cermak, *Diagnosing and Treating Co-Dependence*, 73.

5. Anne Morrow Lindbergh, *Gift from the Sea*, (New York: Pantheon Books, 1955), 24.

6. Marian Perkins, of Saint John, New Brunswick, has stated this concept in relation to codependency.

7. This exercise was adapted from material developed by Lonny Owen of Minneapolis.

CHAPTER 4

*Give us gladness in proportion to our former misery
. . . favor us and give us success.*
— *Psalm 90:15-17*[1]

Your Story and Mine

My Story

There are many different stories of recovery. I have one.
Several members of my extended family had trouble with
alcohol. My mother, a single parent, raised me, and raised me
well. I was sent to the best private schools money could buy.
I went to church, Sunday school, and summer Bible camp.

When I was five years old, I was abducted and molested by
a man in an abandoned church on the block where I lived.

I started drinking to get drunk when I was twelve. The pain
of being me was intense. I had been depressed since age four.
As an adolescent, my memories of hating myself went as far
back as I could remember.

By age thirteen, I was having blackouts. I graduated from
high school on the Twin Cities honor roll, almost a straight A
student. I was a good writer. I was also a chronic over-
achiever and perfectionist. I loved my studies, but no matter
how well I did, I never did "good enough." Once, I had
dreams of someday becoming a writer and newspaper re-
porter, but by the time I graduated from high school, I stopped
expecting anything good from myself or life.

While growing up, on several occasions, prolonged childhood illnesses forced me to bed for a long time. I had one
friend for several years, and another for several months, but
no close friends. I didn't know how to be close to people. I had

deliberately turned my back on God, certain He had done the same to me.

By my twentieth birthday, I was a heroin addict. My relationships with men amounted to a series of victimizations and crazy entanglements with other heroin users. By the time I was twenty-three, I was on the methadone program, a government program that doled out a synthetic substitute for heroin. By the time I was twenty-six, I was committed by the State of Minnesota to the chemical dependency ward of a state hospital. I had a failed marriage and a failed life. I didn't want to stop using chemicals; I wanted to stop living.

Then, something unexpected happened. I decided to give God another chance. He decided to give me another chance. I surrendered. I accepted my powerlessness over chemicals. I saw the unmanageability in my life. I got honest. And I got sober.

I didn't get the program, but it got me.

After eight months, I left the state hospital with much fear, a little hope, and a set of instructions: ask God each morning to help you stay straight that day, thank Him for doing that when you go to bed at night, wait at least two years before going to work in the chemical dependency field, and wait a year to have "a relationship."

I complied with the first three rules. Since my "relationship" didn't work out, I figured I did okay on that one too.

I stayed straight, and in many ways my life improved. Two years after getting sober, I went to work as a chemical dependency and family counselor. I also got married and started having babies.

Seven years after I became sober, my career, relationships, and life stopped working. It didn't matter how long I waited to have a relationship, I didn't know how to have one. I was surrounded by alcoholics. I worked with them; I loved them; I even had some living in my attic. (They didn't want to go to a detoxification center. Could they please learn to stop drinking by living at my house?)

I felt like a perpetual victim. Sobriety became, as a speaker at the Gopher State Round-Up 1986 called it, "a long dark tunnel through which I plodded. And each year a trap door opened and a cake fell through."

I became depressed. One day, I called the local suicide hotline and told a stranger I was thinking about ending my life. I told the counselor I wouldn't really kill myself, because too many people needed me. But I got scared. I had been given a second chance at life, and I didn't know if I wanted it. I didn't know if it was worth living. I didn't know what was wrong. It felt like everyone, including God, had abandoned me. I wondered if I was crazy.

Then, something happened. I learned I wasn't crazy. I learned that, without touching a drop of alcohol, I had been affected by the disease of alcoholism in ways so powerful and baffling it would take me years to fully understand. I stopped resisting and started attending meetings for people effected by alcoholism.

I didn't like it. I resented all those peppy little women running around with smiling faces. But I was there. I started crying. I got honest. And I didn't get the Twelve Step program. But it got me.

I accepted my powerlessness over other people's alcoholism, over other people, over the entire mess my life had become. I saw the unmanageability in my life.

I surrendered. I waved the white flag. I didn't start living happily ever after, but I started living my own life. And that life started to get better.

For years, I trudged through my recovery from codependency, feeling afraid and uncertain about where I was going. But I had faith I was going somewhere different than I had ever before been. I struggled and worked at changing my behaviors — the caretaking, the controlling, the low self-esteem.

I watched myself in relationships and learned how to behave in ways that would leave me feeling less victimized. I learned how to identify what I wanted and then considered that important. I worked on letting go and practicing detachment. I wallowed around in feelings, especially anger, as I came alive emotionally. I learned how to terminate and initiate relationships. I learned how to have fun. I had to make myself do that. It took years.

I've made many mistakes. But I've learned that mistakes are okay too. I learned how to communicate, to laugh, to cry, to ask for help. I'm learning to react less, and act more, quietly confident that who I am is okay.

I've learned to own my power. I've also learned I must constantly return to the act of surrendering to do that.

Recovery from codependency has been the most exciting journey I've taken.

I've learned that self-care isn't narcissistic or indulgent. Self-care is the one thing I can do that most helps me and others too.

My relationships have improved with family, friends, other people, myself, and God. The most difficult matter I've had to face in my recovery was the end of my marriage. Right now, I'm working on the toughest lesson I've ever had to master. I'm learning how to let others love me, and how to allow the "good stuff" to happen in my life. I'm learning how to let God love me. And I'm learning to love, really love, myself.

I can see the many ways I've spent my life sabotaging intimacy, relationships, and myself. I'm changing my behaviors. I'm changing my rules, the powerful messages from the past that control what I do or don't do today. I work aggressively with affirmations. I'm dealing with the host of ways I have been affected by other people and their problems. Sometimes, that means bowing to simple acceptance of what is.

And I'm becoming changed.

Recently, during a radio interview, the host asked me if my life was better now. Of course, I answered, "Yes." But driving home after the interview, I became aware of what I really wanted to say. I wanted to tell him this: "I have many good days. I have some difficult days. But I'm living my life. Is that better? You bet it is. For the first time in my life, I have a life!"

Your Story

Throughout this book, I'll share other people's stories with you. One important story is missing, though. That story is yours.

Twelve Step programs have developed a simple format for telling our story. What was it like? What happened? What's it like now?

People who stop drinking can point to a day on the calendar and say, "There. That's the day I stopped drinking." It's not as easy for us to grab a calendar and say, "There. That's the day I stopped taking care of other people and started taking care of myself!" But try, anyway. How and when did your recovery begin? What got you to that point?

Think about the changes you've made and the changes that have happened to you. What insights have you had? Do you feel good about your progress?

Give some thought to how you've worked at recovery. Which behavior have you struggled with? Name the most difficult thing you've had to deal with in your recovery and tell how you got through that. What's the best thing that happened to you in your recovery? List the things you're working on now. What rewards have you gained? Tell how your life is better and different now.

In the last chapter, I called recovery a process. I said we can trust that process. I want to follow that thought with another one. Not only can we trust the process, we can trust where we're at in it.

Recovery is a healing and a spiritual process. It's also a journey, not a destination. We travel a path from self-neglect into self-responsibility, self-care, and self-love. Like other journeys, it's one of moving forward, taking detours, back-tracking, getting lost, finding the way again, and occasionally stopping to rest. Unlike other journeys, we can't travel it by forcing the next foot forward. It's a gentle journey, traveled by discipline, and by accepting and celebrating where we are in that journey today.

Where we are today is where we're meant to be. It's where we need to be to get where we're going tomorrow. And that place we're going tomorrow will be better than any we've been before.

Activity

1. Write your story. At an appropriate time and place, share your story with someone safe.

2. Pat yourself on the back for what you've accomplished.

ENDNOTES

1. *The Living Bible* (Wheaton, Ill.: Tyndale House Publishers, 1971), 481.

SECTION II

RELAPSE

Maybe we shouldn't call relapse "recycling."
Maybe we should call it "cycles of growth."
Or maybe we should just call it
"growth."

CHAPTER 5

"Tell me about the reality of recovery," I said. "Oh, that," she replied. "You mean two steps forward and one step back."

— *Anonymous*

Recycling: The Relapse Process

"I did it again," Jan confided. "And I did it ten years after I began my recovery from codependency.

"Steve and I are divorced. He hasn't paid child support in six months because he's drinking and not working, and I handed him $250 of my hard-earned money — probably to get drunk on.

"I'm furious! I can't believe I let him do that to me. I know better. I didn't want to do it. I let him bully and guilt me out of the money."

Jan took a deep breath and continued. "Afterward, I drove over to his apartment and demanded the money back. I made a fool of myself, screaming and stomping around.

"I feel angry, depressed, and ashamed. Sometimes I think I don't know anything about recovery. I called my sponsor and whined to her. All those meetings! All that therapy! All that work! Didn't it mean anything? I was still caretaking. Still allowing people to use me. And still stomping around acting crazy.

I asked Jan what her sponsor said. "She said at least I was asking why I was allowing people to use me, instead of asking why they were doing this to me," Jan said. "And she said at least I could recognize when my behavior was crazy."

Over the years, I've seen people use different diagrams to represent the recovery or growth process. I've seen recovery portrayed as a zig-zagging line moving upward and forward, with each zig forming a higher peak than the last. (See Diagram 1, page 47)[1] I've seen recovery drawn as a circular line moving inward in smaller circles until an inner core of stability is reached; an inner core large enough to permit continued growth. (See Diagram 2.)[2] I've seen recovery diagramed as a line moving upward and forward, making repetitively-spinning circles on the way, cyclical but forward-moving. (See Diagram 3.)[3] One diagram I haven't seen drawn to represent recovery is a straight line upward and forward. (See Diagram 4.) Recovery is not this.

Recovery is a process. Within that process is another one called relapse. Regression, reverting, slips — whatever we call it — any diagram we use to represent growth needs to accommodate it.

In spite of our best efforts to stay on track, we sometimes find ourselves reverting to old ways of thinking, feeling, and behaving, even when we know better.

Relapse can sneak up on us, linger, and become as confusing as our original codependency. Or it can be brief. Sometimes, we're reacting to other people's craziness. Sometimes, we're reacting to ourselves. Sometimes, we're reacting to the years of training we've had in how to be codependent. Sometimes, we're just reacting.

For many reasons, we can find ourselves using coping behaviors we thought we had outgrown. We start neglecting ourselves, taking care of others, feeling victimized, freezing feelings, overreacting, trying to control, feeling dependent and needy, guilty, afraid, obligated, depressed, deprived, undeserving, and trapped. The codependent crazies come back, and we feel neck deep in shame.

No need to feel shame. I've questioned thousands of recovering people. No one claimed a perfect recovery.

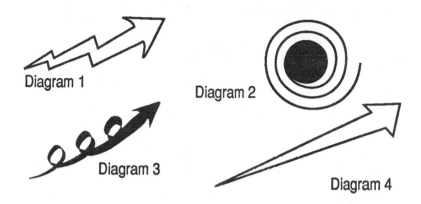

Diagram 1

Diagram 2

Diagram 3

Diagram 4

"I thought something awful was wrong with me," recalls Charlene. "I kept threatening to leave my boyfriend, but I didn't leave him. I felt disconnected from people — all alone in the world. I got irritable, depressed, and couldn't sleep. I thought I was dying. I went to the doctor. He said I was fine, but I didn't feel fine. This went on for months before I realized it was my codependency. I got really scared. It took some work, but now I'm back on track again."

Jack tells this story: "Last weekend my friend's wife called me. I'm recovering from chemical addiction and codependency. My friend is still drinking, and his wife is still thinking about going to Al-Anon. She planned to leave town for the weekend and asked me to stay with her husband while she was gone. She said *he* really wanted to stay sober that weekend and *he* wanted to go fishing with me. I agreed. When I arrived, I realized her husband had no intention of going fishing. He wanted to go drinking. She set me up to be his baby-sitter for the weekend. I felt tricked and trapped. It was one of the most miserable weekends I've had in my two years of recovery. And I couldn't open my mouth and get out. I had a big slip, a codependency slip."

Marilyn tells this story: "I was recovering for five years

when I moved in with Bob, a recovering alcoholic. One year later, I found myself living with a nondrinking alcoholic who had stopped attending his recovery meetings. I started feeling crazy again. I felt guilty, insecure, needy, and resentful. It happened gradually. I just slid into it. I stopped setting boundaries. I quit asking for what I wanted and needed. I stopped saying, 'No!' I stopped taking care of myself. I couldn't figure out what was wrong. Then one day, when I was considering ending the relationship, I found myself thinking, *No! I can't do that. I can't live without him.* That thought jolted me into awareness and action. I know better than that!"

Relapse happens to many of us. Relapse happens to people who have been recovering for ten months or ten years. It happens not because we're deficient or lackadaisical. Relapse happens because it's a normal part of the recovery process.

In fact, it's so normal I'm not going to call it relapse. I'm going to call it "recycling."[4]

Relapse, according to the New World Dictionary, means to slip or fall back into a former condition after improvement or *seeming* improvement.[5] *Recycle* means to recover; or to pass through a cycle or part of a cycle again for checking or treating.[6]

"Relapse sounds like going all the way back to where we started from — square one on the game board," explains my friend, Scott Egleston, who is also a therapist. "We don't go all the way back. When we finish a recycling process, we move to a progressed location on our recovery journey."

Recycling is more than a normal part of recovery. Sometimes, it's a necessary part. For example, in the beginning of this chapter, Jan talked about allowing her ex-husband to bully her out of money. Her story has an epilogue. About four months after the incident, Jan was having coffee with her sponsor. Her sponsor asked Jan if she had learned anything from the incident.

"By then, I had learned something from it," Jan said,

"something valuable. That incident was part of a larger, important lesson I was in the midst of learning. Financially, I was finally getting on my feet, and I was starting to leave behind the sick people in my life. I was standing up to the bullying, and I was letting go of the guilt about becoming healthy. The lesson I was learning involved the idea that I could feel compassion for people without acting on it."

All our recycling incidents can have epilogues. We can gain from them when they happen. Recycling is a chance to do our recovery work. It's a way to discover what we need to work on and work through. It's one way we figure out what we haven't yet learned, so we can start to learn that. It's a way to solidify what we've already learned, so we continue to know that. Recycling is about learning our lessons so we can move forward on our journey.

Activity

1. What would a diagram of your recovery look like?

2. As you progress through this book, you may want to start accumulating a list of affirmations. Some suggestions for affirmations on recycling would be:

- My recovery history is okay. All my experiences are necessary and valuable.
- I am learning what I need to know. I will learn what I need to when the time is right.
- I am right where I need to be.

ENDNOTES

1. This is a diagram often used to represent recovery from chemical addiction, recovery from codependency, and recovery and growth.

2. Scott Egleston and others have used this to diagram codependency and recovery.

3. Lonny Owen used this to diagram recovery from codependency. He got the idea from someone else, who got the idea from another. . . .

4. Scott Egleston suggested this term.

5. *New World Dictionary of the American Language, Second College Edition* (New York, Simon & Schuster, Inc., 1984), 1198.

6. *New World Dictionary of the American Language, Second College Edition* (New York, Simon & Schuster, Inc., 1984), 1189.

CHAPTER 6

"Thank you for writing Codependent Once
More. *Oops! Freudian slip. I mean,* Codependent
No More.*"*[1]

Common Recycling Situations

Society is filled with invitations to be codependent, Anne
Wilson Schaef once said.[2] And, if we don't get invited, we
may invite ourselves. In this chapter, we'll explore some of
these situations.

Recycling on the Job

We can recycle at work for many reasons. Sometimes, we
bring our behaviors with us. If we're still trying to control
people at home, we may be doing the same at work. If we're
not setting boundaries at home, we may not be doing it at
work either. Sometimes, we've acquired self-care skills at
home and in personal relationships, but we haven't learned
how to take care of ourselves on the job and in professional
relationships.

Other times, issues at work can point to a larger issue we
need to address. "I haven't been happy about my job," says
Alice, who has been recovering from codependency for many
years. "I've been complaining and whining about it. So I
decided to go see a counselor, and during counseling a new
awareness struck me.

"I don't like my job. I took it because it met my parents'
standards. I've stayed because they wouldn't approve of me
leaving. I can hear them: 'All those benefits? All that senior-
ity? You're going to walk away and leave all that?'

"Yes," Alice says, "that's exactly what I'm going to do."

Sometimes, we find ourselves working with an alcoholic or other troubled person. An addicted person can inflict as much chaos at work as he or she can at home.

When a prestigious hospital offered Marlyss a job, she was delighted. She had put herself through nursing school in mid-life. Eight years ago, she began recovering from codependency, and developing her career was a big part of that. But two and a half years after she started working at the hospital, Marlyss was feeling crazy again.

"I finally figured out what was happening," she says. "I had been promoted to a supervisory position. My supervisor was a practicing alcoholic. The nurses under my supervision were reacting to my alcoholic supervisor and the crazy system. I was reacting to everyone — my supervisor and the nurses I supervised. I was in my familiar role of peacemaker and caretaker, feeling responsible for everyone and everything. It was like the family system at home used to be. And I felt like I used to — real codependent."

Marlyss began to practice detachment at work. After a while, she found a different job. She's worked there three years now. "I love it," Marlyss says. "Moving on was one of the best moves I ever made."

Some people may find themselves employed by abusive or abrasive people. "My boss treated me so nasty," Ella says. "He was verbally abusive. He made sexual innuendos. I had been recovering from codependency for several years, and it still took me months to realize I wasn't doing something wrong; he was."

Jerry, a recovering codependent and alcoholic who owned his own business, had the following experience. "I hired a secretary. She was great, at first," Jerry recalls. "She was willing to learn and work hard. Before long, I discovered she was married to an alcoholic. At first I felt sorry for her, then I got mad. Whenever he was doing too much drinking, she didn't want to stay home. She worked late and weekends, and charged me overtime. It was taking her longer than it should to get her work done. She was making a lot of mistakes at my expense.

"I didn't say much at first. I suggested she go to Al-Anon, but she wasn't ready. I felt ashamed about getting angry. She really did have it hard, married to an alcoholic. But I could also see how she kept setting herself up to be used by the guy. I got angrier and angrier, then the pieces started to fit. I've stopped feeling sorry for her and started taking care of myself. I know it's a myth that codependents are sicker than alcoholics. I know how much codependents hurt; I am one. But I'm also beginning to see how difficult it can be to deal with one. You can get just as codependent on a codependent as you can on an alcoholic."

A family is a system with its own rules, roles, and personality. And employment settings can be similar. Sometimes a person in that system is dysfunctional. Sometimes, the system is dysfunctional, either covertly or overtly.

"I had been recovering for about two years when I went to work for a radio station," says Al, an adult child of an alcoholic. "I really wanted the job. I still do. But boy, did it hook my codependency. We're a small station on a small budget with a small staff and a large mission — doing all we can to save the city.

"After I'd been working there a couple of months, I noticed many of my codependency symptoms reappearing. This time it wasn't about my relationship; it was about my job. I was working sixty hours a week, neglecting myself, feeling like no matter how much I did it wasn't enough. I was feeling irritable, angry, and guilty because I couldn't do more. Whenever I considered setting boundaries or taking care of myself, I felt more guilt. How could I be so selfish? Who would do it, if I didn't? What about our mission? There wasn't enough of me to go around. Now, I'm figuring out how to take care of myself in this organization."

Sally found herself in a difficult employment situation. She took a management position in a sales force several years after beginning recovery from chemical dependency and codependency. Within six months, she started feeling "nuts" again. "Just like in the old days," Sally says.

"Company policy surpassed high-pressure selling. It involved unethical practices. The company used people — employees and customers. I didn't feel comfortable following company policy. For a while, I tried to pretend I did. Then, pretending got too hard. I talked to my supervisor. He understood, but company policy was company policy. By then, I had learned you can't change other people. Now, I was learning you can't change a corporation either. The only thing left was to change myself. I did. I changed jobs."

For years, Earnie Larsen, a respected author and lecturer on recovery issues, has preached that some systems demand sick behavior from the people in it. He was talking about families, but employment systems can be just as demanding.

Sometimes, recycling at work is a clue to something we need to work on or through. Other times, it's an indicator of how much we've grown. We often choose relationships that are about as healthy as we are and meet our current (but changing) needs; we often choose jobs in the same way. We can grow out of relationships; we can grow out of jobs.

"I took a job during the first year of my recovery from codependency," Kelly says. "I was devastated at the time, crushed by a sick relationship that had gone on for years. At first, the job felt good. It was a safe place to be. The work wasn't demanding, but it kept me busy. And the people were nice. I felt like I fit in."

After about eighteen months, Kelly's feelings about her job changed. She felt out of place. She started repressing feelings, going numb at work.

"I don't know how or when it happened, but I realized I no longer fit in. The healthier I became, the more I saw many of my co-workers were victims. And they wanted me to be a victim. As I grew and did more things to take care of myself, they got angry at me. I felt torn. I wanted to fit in and be part of the crowd. But I didn't want to be a victim."

Although Kelly has decided to stay at her job for a while, she says she suspects she'll soon move on. She's been recovering long enough to know change isn't necessarily bad. It can bring us to our next plateau of growth.

Other systems besides employment settings can invite us to behave codependently. We can recycle at church, in recovery groups, and in social, professional, or charitable associations. Wherever people gather, the possibility of us using our codependent coping behaviors exists.

"I went to church on Sunday feeling good. I left feeling ashamed. I never felt good enough, no matter what I did," says Len, a recovering codependent. "I constantly felt pressured into volunteering for things. I couldn't tell if I was giving money because I wanted to or because I felt guilty. I was fine all week. But I felt crazy in church.

"I've since switched churches. I need to hear God loves me, not that He's waiting to punish me. I've lived with fear and condemnation all my life. Looking back, I think that church was as shame based as my family." I just didn't realize it until I got healthier.

We can recycle in therapy or support groups too. "I knew I was an alcoholic and needed A.A. I also knew I was codependent and needed Al-Anon," says Theresa. "But members of my A.A. group started giving me a hard time. They said if I was really working a good A.A. program, I wouldn't need Al-Anon.

"I dropped out of Al-Anon, and started feeling real crazy again. Then I realized the people in my A.A. group didn't have to approve of me dealing with my codependency. Either they didn't understand, or they were uncomfortable with my attendance in Al-Anon. I didn't need to figure them out; my job was to take care of myself."

Taking care of ourselves may mean finding another job, church, or group. Or, it may mean figuring out how to function in the job, church, or group we're in. Theresa has continued attending the same A.A. group. She also continues to attend Al-Anon.

Recycling in Relationships

Recycling is possible and fairly predictable in any relationship. We can give up our power and get crazy with people we've known for years and with strangers. We can start reacting to people we love and people we're not certain we like.

We can start feeling guilty, as if we are at fault, when others behave inappropriately. Sometimes, we recycle without any help from them at all.

Sometimes we need to learn to use certain recovery skills that we've acquired in one kind of relationship — for instance, our special love relationship — in another kind of relationship — for instance, a friendship.

"I can set boundaries with my husband and children. I'm lousy at setting boundaries with friends," says one woman.

We can react to new people in our lives — people whose addiction or problem catches us off guard. Or we can react to people whose addiction or dysfunction we know all too well.

"I can be going along just fine," says Sarah. "But after ten minutes on the phone with my ex-husband, I'm a basket case again. I still try to trust him. I still go into denial about his alcoholism. I still get hooked into shame and guilt when I talk to him. It's taken me a long time, but I'm finally learning I don't have to talk to him. The same thing happens each time."

Sometimes, past relationships hold important lessons. We may need to go back long enough to realize we don't want to stay.

Family reunions, holidays, and other family gatherings can challenge our recovery. Besides triggering a reaction to whatever is happening that day, it can trigger old feelings.

Dealing with family members, whether they're in recovery or not, can be provocative. "I get trapped on the phone with family members," explains Linda. "I can feel myself going through the whole process, feeling enraged, guilty, then going numb. They're not in recovery. They go on and on. I tell them I have to go, but they don't listen. Short of hanging up, I don't know what to do!

"Sometimes it leaves me feeling drained for hours. I get so angry. My family is important to me. I'd like to tape record those conversations and make them listen to themselves for endless hours, like I do.

"I've been recovering from codependency for eight years. I know the answer isn't making other people listen to themselves and 'see the light.' The solution is me listening to myself and me 'seeing the light.' Sometimes I can cope with my family, but sometimes, I still get tangled up with them."

We may find ourselves periodically, or cyclically, reacting to certain people in our lives. "I've noticed my recycling in relationships comes in cycles. I'm fine for a few months, then it feels like crazy people come crawling out of the woodwork. It's usually the same people, and they seem determined to inflict their insanity on me, all at the same time," says one woman. "I don't understand it. But I do understand this: it becomes time to detach and take care of myself."

Dealing with children can challenge our recovery. "I'm good at taking care of myself with the rest of the world. But with my kids, I feel guilty when I say no. I feel guilty when I feel angry at them. I feel guilty about disciplining them. I allow them to treat me terribly, then I'm the one who feels guilty!" says one woman.

"My son has admitted he deliberately uses guilt-producing tactics on me. In his weaker moments, he calls it 'the guilt trap.' He's admitted he compares me to other mothers and lies about what they're letting their kids do to control me. My kids know what they're doing. It's about time I learn what I need to do," she concludes.

"Setting boundaries with my children is harder for me than setting limits at work, with friends, or with my girlfriend," says a divorced man. "I feel so guilty when I do, and so victimized when I don't."

Dealing with other people's children can be more difficult than dealing with our own. I've asked recovering people, "What's the hardest part of your relationship?" Many people in relationships involving children from past marriages say, "Dealing with the children."

But the greatest challenge to our recoveries still seems to be our special love relationships. "I don't know how to be in love and not be codependent," says a recovering woman. "I was friends for over a year with a man. The minute we moved in together, we both stopped taking care of ourselves and tried to control each other. It really got nuts. When I'm in love, anything goes. And what usually goes first is my recovery behaviors."

We can get uncomfortable when a relationship gets too close and too good. Crisis and chaos may not feel good, but those things can feel comfortable. Sometimes, we get so anxious waiting for the formidable other shoe to drop that we take it off and toss it ourselves.

"I'm in a good relationship, one with tremendous potential," says a recovering woman. "We get along great, but whenever things get too good, I create a problem. At first, I couldn't see this was my pattern. I thought things just got good, then bad. Now, I'm starting to see my part."

There are many reasons for recycling in relationships. Sometimes the relationship is over, but we're not ready to end it. Sometimes the relationship needs to be enjoyed, but we're too frightened to do that. Sometimes we're making chaos to avoid intimacy. Sometimes falling in love can resemble codependency; as boundaries weaken, we focus on the other person and have a sense of loss of control. Sometimes what we call "codependent behaviors" are a normal part of intimate or close relationships.

Relationships are where we take our recovery show on the road. Taking good care of ourselves doesn't mean we avoid relationships. The goal of recovery is learning how to function in relationships. The task during recycling is to relax and let ourselves learn whatever we need to learn.

Other Recycling Situations

Many other circumstances can provoke our codependency. Sometimes we begin denying that codependency is real and recovery is our responsibility. We may neglect our recoveries and stop taking care of ourselves. Sometimes we neglect ourselves before a recycling incident; sometimes we do it after we begin recycling, making things worse.

"How long do I need to keep working at recovery?" asks one woman. "All my life, I guess," she says, answering her own question. "Whenever I stop taking my recovery seriously, my life gets crazy again."

Sometimes our old reactions appear for *no reason*.

Sometimes recycling is part of the experimental process we go through as we struggle to acquire new behaviors and shed old, self-defeating ones.

Getting sick or becoming overly tired can trigger codependent reactions in us. Stress — from today and yesterday — can trigger our codependency. Our instinctive reaction to stressful situations can be to neglect ourselves.

Innocuous events that remind us of past traumatic events can also trigger our codependency.

"Once a person has been overwhelmed by traumatic events, he or she is susceptible to the sudden reemergence of the feelings, thoughts, and behaviors that were present during the trauma," Cermak writes in *Diagnosing and Treating Co-Dependence*. "This reemergence is most likely to occur when the individual is faced with something which symbolically represents the original trauma — a 'trigger.' "[3]

Triggers remind our subconscious of a traumatic event, causing codependent feelings and behaviors to emerge. This can include

- feeling anxious or afraid;
- freezing feelings, or "going numb";
- focusing on others and neglecting ourselves;
- attempting to control things, events, and people;
- experiencing sudden low self-worth;
- or any of the codependent behaviors or feelings we did or felt during the actual event.

We automatically start reacting and protecting ourselves.

We each have our own triggers. If it was connected to something frightening or distressing that happened before, it can be a trigger now.

Almost anything can be a trigger:

- conflict;
- the threat of someone leaving us, even if we want him or her to leave;
- confrontation;
- paying bills;
- or hearing a certain song.

Anything connected with, resembling, or representing a past traumatic experience can be a trigger. Falling in love can resemble codependency; it can trigger it too.

Understanding our triggers may not make these sudden resurgences of codependency disappear, but understanding can help us get out more swiftly.

"Paying bills is a trigger for me," says Carol. "I've got enough money now. That's not the problem. The problem is all the years I was married to an alcoholic, and there wasn't enough money. Before I learned about my triggers, I felt anxious and distressed the day I paid the bills. Now, I recognize what's happening. I still get skittish, but I tell myself it's okay. There's enough money now. And there's going to be enough."

Problems and trauma aren't the only matters that can provoke codependency. Success, in any area of our lives, can cause us to start controlling and caretaking again.

"I know how to cope with emergencies, tragedy, and disappointment," confides a recovering woman. "I don't know how to deal with success, peace, and loving relationships. Those things are uncomfortable. I get scared. I wonder what bad thing is going to happen next. Some terrible thing always did in the past. It's difficult for me to believe I deserve good things. It's even harder for me to believe good things can last."

Changing circumstances can cause us to recycle. Changing jobs, moving, ending a relationship, the threat of ending a relationship, a change in finances, or a shift in routine can be unnerving. Even desirable change brings a sense of loss. Most of us have been through so much change and loss that we don't want to go through any more.

About six months after *Codependent No More* was released, my life began to change. I was working for a newspaper and doing free-lance writing on weekends and evenings. Requests for me to speak began filtering in. I was shuffling all this into the routine of being the single parent of two young children. I was also trying to stay involved in my own recovery process and find time to have fun.

My life kept filling up with new activities. I kept trying to hang on to the old ones and make room for the new. I kept waiting for things to go back to normal. What I didn't realize was normal had changed.

Then I got sick with double pneumonia. I learned of the diagnosis twenty-four hours before I was scheduled to speak in Joplin, Missouri. I thought it would be inappropriate to cancel that close to the event, so I pushed myself through. When I returned to Minnesota, I had several stories due at the paper. I told myself I couldn't cancel that either.

I spent a day struggling to grind out a story that ordinarily would have taken me three hours. After eight hours, I hadn't yet produced the first paragraph. I stayed late, hoping the quiet would help me think more clearly. By eight o'clock that night, I had wrestled out four or five paragraphs.

When I went to the lounge to take a break, I heard that still voice within me. It said: *It's time to take care of yourself.* I was running around the country, preaching those words. I had written a book carrying that message. Now, it was time to listen to myself.

When we start feeling the codependent crazies again, we know what time it is. It's time to take care of ourselves.

Whether we recycle or not, we can benefit by putting extra attention into self-care during these circumstances. And whether we're reacting to a crazy system, a person, ourselves, our pasts, or just reacting, taking care of ourselves remains a "no-fault" issue. It's our responsibility.

Somewhere between our first response — shaking our finger at the other person and saying, "It's your fault" — and our second reaction — pointing that finger at ourselves and wondering, *What's wrong with me?* — there's a lesson to learn. That lesson is ours to learn.

Activity

1. Did any recycling incidents come to mind as you read this chapter? How did you take care of yourself in that situation?

2. Do any people in your life seem to particularly trigger your codependency? Who? What happens? What are some ways you can start taking care of yourself with these people?

3. As you go through your daily routine, watch for your "triggers." What things seem to engage those old codependent feelings "for no reason"? Look for the reason, the connection to the past. When that happens, what can you tell yourself to help yourself feel better?

ENDNOTES

1. This is an edited quote from a letter I received from an anonymous woman in New South Wales, Australia.

2. Schaef made this comment when we both appeared on a radio show, via the telephone.

3. Timmen L. Cermak, M.D., *Diagnosing and Treating Co-Dependence* (Minneapolis: Johnson Institute, 1986), 55.

CHAPTER 7

I still have bad days, but that's okay. I used to have bad years.

— Anonymous

Getting Through The Cycle

Recycling can mean a momentary lapse into our old behaviors. Or recycling can lead to more serious problems: depression, use of mood-altering chemicals to cope, or physical illness. Codependency is progressive; recycling can be too. We can get stuck, spin our wheels, then discover we've gotten ourselves more deeply entrenched in the muck.

Whether our recycling experience lasts six minutes or six months, our instinctive reaction is usually one of denial, shame, and self-neglect. That's not the way out. That's the way in more deeply.

We get out of, or through, a recycling process by practicing acceptance, self-compassion, and self-care. These attitudes and behaviors may not come as effortlessly as denial, shame, and neglect. We've spent years practicing denial, shame, and neglect. But we can learn to practice healthier alternatives, even when it feels awkward. Some suggestions for doing that follow.

Practicing Healthier Alternatives

The first step toward getting through a recycling situation is identifying when we're in it. Here are some warning signs.[1]

Emotions Shut Down. We may go numb and begin freezing or ignoring feelings. We return to the mind set that feelings are unnecessary, inappropriate, unjustified, or unimportant. We may tell ourselves the same things about wants and needs.

Compulsive Behaviors Return. We may begin compulsively eating, caretaking, controlling, working, staying busy, spending money, engaging in sexual behaviors, or anything else we compulsively do to avoid feeling.

Victim Self-Image Returns. We may start feeling, thinking, talking, and acting like a victim again. We may begin focusing on others, or resort to blaming and scapegoating. A good clue that I'm "in it" is when I hear myself whining about how someone is doing this or that to me, or how awful something is. My voice begins to grate on my nerves.

Self-Worth Drops. Our level of self-esteem may drop. We may get stuck in self-hatred or shame. We may become overly critical of ourselves and others. Perfectionism and feelings of not being good enough may return.

Self-Neglect Starts. Neglecting the small and large acts of self-care that are a regular part of our recovery routine may indicate we're close to a recycling situation. Abandoning our daily routine is another sign.

The Crazies Return. All the old crud can come back. This includes: return of anxiety and fear; feeling disconnected from people and our Higher Power; problems sleeping (too much or too little); mind-racing; feeling overwhelmed by confusion (or just overwhelmed); difficulty thinking clearly; feeling angry and resentful; feeling guilty because we feel that way; feeling desperate, depressed, deprived, undeserving, and unloved. We may get into the "overs": overtired, overworked, overcommitted, overextended, overly sensitive; or the "unders": underpaid, underappreciated, underspent, underfed, and under-the-weather.

A continuing physical condition can be a warning sign that something is nagging at our minds and emotions. We may begin withdrawing from and avoiding people. A return to martyrdom or the "endurance mode" is another warning sign. This would include resuming the belief that we can't enjoy life or have fun today, this week, or this month; life is something to be "gotten through," and maybe next week or next year we can be happy.

The Behaviors Return Too. Once we're into a recycling situation, any or all the coping behaviors may return.

Trapped! Feeling trapped, believing we have no choices, is a highly suspect attitude.

Not That Again. It's possible to progress to the danger zone during recycling. Symptoms here include chronic physical illness, chemical dependency, chronic depression, or possible fantasies about suicide.

After we've identified a return to our old ways, the next step is simple. We say, "Oops! I'm doing it again." This is called *acceptance and honesty*. It's helpful to return to concepts like powerlessness and unmanageability at this time. If we're working a Twelve Step program, this is a good time to work Step One. This is called "surrender." Now comes the potentially difficult part. We tell ourselves, *It's okay, I did it again.* This is called "self-compassion."

Recycling Myths

Believing any of the following myths about recycling may make recovery more difficult than necessary.

● I should be further along than I am.
● If I've been recovering for a number of years, I shouldn't be having problems with this anymore.
● If I was working a good program, I wouldn't be doing this.
● If I'm a professional in the recovery, mental health, or general helping field, I shouldn't be having this problem.
● If my recovery was real, I wouldn't be doing this.
● People wouldn't respect me if they knew I thought, felt, or did this.
● Once changed, a behavior is gone forever.
● I couldn't possibly be doing this again. I know better.
● Oh, no! I'm back to square one.

These are myths. If we believe them, we need to try to

change what we believe. It's okay to have problems. It's okay to recycle. People who work good programs and have good recoveries recycle, even if they're professionals. It's okay to do "it" again, even when we know better. We haven't gone all the way back to square one. Who knows? We may learn from it this time.

If we insist on blaming or feeling ashamed, we can give ourselves a limited time to do that. Five to fifteen minutes should be enough.

Taking Care of Ourselves

After we've accepted ourselves and given ourselves a hug, we ask ourselves two questions.

- "What do I need to do to take care of myself?"
- "What am I supposed to learn?"

Often, the self-care concepts we need to practice are basic:

- acceptance,
- surrender,
- realistic evaluation of what we can control,
- detachment,
- removing the victim,
- dealing with feelings,
- taking what we want and need seriously,
- setting boundaries,
- making choices and taking responsibility for them,
- setting goals,
- getting honest,
- letting go, and
- giving ourselves huge doses of love and nurturing.

Consciously focusing on our recovery program, talking to healthy people, plying ourselves with meditations and positive thoughts, relaxing, and doing fun activities help too.

We need to get our balance back.

Taking care of ourselves at work may require some different

considerations than caring for ourselves at home. Certain behaviors may be appropriate at home but could result in loss of our job. We may not want to tell the boss how mad we are at him. Self-care is self-responsibility.

Codependency is a self-defeating cycle. Codependent feelings lead to self-neglect, self-neglect leads to more codependent feelings and behaviors, leading to more self-neglect, and around we go. Recovery is a more energizing cycle. Self-care leads to better feelings, healthier feelings lead to more self-care, and around that track we travel.

I don't know precisely what you need to do to take care of yourself. But I know you can figure it out.

Another thing I don't know is what lesson you're learning. It's all I can do to learn my own. I can't tell you how to make sense of the particular experiences in your life, but I can tell you this: between you and your Higher Power, you will figure that out too.

Don't worry. If you don't understand, or if you aren't ready to learn your lesson today, that's okay. Lessons don't go away. They keep presenting themselves until we learn them. And we'll do that when we're ready and the time is right.[2]

Recycling Tips

Although I don't have a formula for self-care and learning life's lessons, I've collected some tips that may help during recycling.

- If it feels crazy, it probably is. Often when we run into a crazy system, our first reaction is still to wonder what's wrong with us. We can trust some people, but we can't trust everyone. We can trust ourselves.
- If we're protecting ourselves, something may be threatening us. Maybe a trigger is reminding us of the old days or an old message is sabotaging us. Sometimes, someone in our present is threatening us, and we're trying to pretend

they're not. If we're protecting ourselves, it helps to understand who or what is scaring us, and what we're protecting ourselves from.

- When one method of problem solving fails, try another. Sometimes, we get stuck. We encounter a problem, decide to solve it a certain way, fail, then repeatedly, sometimes for years, try to solve that problem in the same way, even though that way doesn't work. Regroup and try something else.
- Self-will doesn't work any better during recovery than it did before. Surrendering does work. Sometimes in recycling, we're going through the process of denying a problem that's creeping into our awareness. We're struggling to avoid it or overcome it by exerting greater amounts of self-will. When self-will fails, try surrender.
- Feelings of guilt, pity, and obligation are to the codependent as the first drink is to the alcoholic. Watch out for what happens next.
- Feeling sad and frustrated because we can't control someone or something is not the same as controlling.[3]
- Trying to recoup our losses generally doesn't work. "If I look back and stare at my losses too long, they gain on me," says one man. "I've learned to take them and run."
- We cannot simultaneously set a boundary and take care of the other person's feelings.[4]
- Today isn't yesterday. Things change.
- We don't have to do more today than we can reasonably do. If we're tired, rest. If we need to play, play. The work will get done.
- When depressed, look to see if anger, shame, or guilt is present.[5]
- If we're not certain, we can wait.
- It's hard to feel compassion for someone while that person is using or victimizing us. We'll probably feel angry. First, we stop allowing ourselves to be used. Then, we work

toward compassion. Anger can motivate us to set bound-aries, but we don't need to stay resentful to keep taking care of ourselves.

- If we listen to ourselves, we'll probably hear ourselves say what the problem is. The next step is acceptance.
- We never outgrow our need for nurturing and self-care.
- If everything looks black, we've probably got our eyes shut.

When all else fails, try gratitude. Sometimes, that's what we're supposed to be learning. If we can't think of anything to be grateful about, be grateful anyway. Will gratitude. Fake it if necessary. Sometimes in recycling, we need to change something we're doing. Sometimes things are being worked out in us, important intangibles that may not be clear for months or years, things like patience, faith, and self-esteem.

"I've had a lot of ups and downs, a lot of pain, and a lot of loss," says one woman. "I'm still not sure what everything's been about, but I've learned a few things. I've learned where I live, what I wear, and where I work isn't me. I'm me. And no matter what happens, I can land on my feet."

Come to think of it, maybe we shouldn't call relapse "re-cycling." Maybe we should call it "cycles of growth." Or maybe we should just call it "growth."

Recycling, getting stuck, bad days, whatever we call it, can be tough, especially if we've had a taste of better days. We can frighten ourselves, worrying that all the old stuff is back again, maybe to stay. We don't have to worry. We don't have to go all the way back. The old stuff isn't here to stay. It's part of the process, and in that process, some days go better than others. We can count them all for joy.

Lonny Owen[6] and I conducted a ten-week workshop and support group for "advanced codependents" (those of us who know better, but do it anyway). All the participants had previously identified themselves as codependents; all had been actively involved in recovery for at least a year. Most had been working at recovery much longer. We bypassed the business of "Am I codependent? Maybe I'm not? What is codependency anyway?" We got down to the core of the matter: "Where am I stuck in my recovery? What am I stuck on? And what do I need to do to improve my life and my relationships?"

The workshop required much vulnerability from the participants. They were asked to expose themselves, to be honest about who they were when they had been recovering that long. The group also required some vulnerability from Lonny and me. This time we weren't working with "beginning" codependents. We were working with people who had a good deal of information about the subject we were teaching. In other words, we were scared too.

It was the most challenging group I've facilitated in my thirteen-plus years in and around the recovery field. It was also the most exciting. I saw more growth accomplished in ten weeks than I've seen in any similar group.

Want to know how we did it? First, let me tell you what we didn't do. We didn't criticize, judge, condemn, confront, blame, or shame. Of course, the participants' commitment and courage to grow made their growth possible. But the growth in that group happened because we stuck to concepts like honesty, acceptance, nurturing, affirmation, approval, empowerment, and love.

That's how we did our work. You can too.

Activity

1. What are your patterns of self-neglect when you get into a recycling situation? For example, mine include: eliminating fun activities, neglecting proper nutrition, and pushing harder when the problem is I've pushed too hard.

2. What are some of your favorite acts of self-care, activities that help you feel good about yourself? What are some things you enjoyed doing for yourself when you began your recovery from codependency that you've stopped doing? What is your rationale for not doing those things anymore?[7]

3. Look over the recovery checklist that follows. This checklist can help you determine your strengths and weaknesses in recovery. It can also be helpful in setting your recovery goals.

Recovery Check List[8]

___ Maintaining appropriate daily routine
___ Setting and achieving daily and long-term goals
___ Personal care
___ Setting and sticking to limits with children and others
___ Constructive planning
___ Appropriate decision-making and problem-solving efforts
___ Choosing behaviors
___ Well-rested
___ Resentment-free
___ Accepting (versus denying)
___ Not controlling others nor feeling controlled by them
___ Open to appropriate criticism and feedback
___ Free of excessive criticism of self and others
___ Gratitude versus self-pity and deprivation
___ Responsible financial decisions (not over- or underspending)
___ Appropriate nutrition (not over- or undereating)
___ Not escaping or avoiding through work or sex
___ Self-responsibility (versus scapegoating and blaming)
___ Valuing wants and needs
___ Free of victim self-image
___ Free of fear and anxiety
___ Free of guilt and shame
___ Free of worry and obsession
___ Not feeling excessively responsible for others
___ Faith in Higher Power
___ Trusting and valuing self
___ Making appropriate decisions about trusting others
___ Maintaining recovery routine (attending support groups, et cetera)

___ Mind clear and peaceful; logical thinking; free of confusion

___ Feeling and dealing appropriately with feelings, including anger

___ Appropriately disclosing

___ Reasonable expectations of self and others

___ Needing people versus NEEDING them

___ Feeling secure with self; self-affirming

___ Communicating clearly, directly, and honestly

___ Balanced mood

___ Maintaining contact with friends

___ Feeling connected and close to people versus lonely and isolated

___ Healthy perspective; life looks worth living

___ Not using alcohol and medication to cope

___ Having fun, relaxing during leisure activities, enjoying daily routine

___ Giving appropriate positive feedback to self and others

___ Getting — and allowing self to believe — positive feedback

ENDNOTES

1. These signs are based in part on "Co-Alcoholic Relapse: Family Factors and Warning Signs," Terence T. Gorski and Merlene Miller, from *Co-dependency, An Emerging Issue* (Pompano Beach, Fla.: Health Communications, Inc., 1984), 82.

2. Based in part on an interview with Donna Wallace, "Donna Wallace on Empowering ACoAs at Work," *Phoenix* 8, no. 5 (May 1988): 2.

3. This is wisdom from Scott Egleston.

4. I got this wisdom from a woman I met at an airport. I neglected to get her name, but she travels across the country teaching nurses about codependency, bases much of her teaching on *Codependent No More*, and shared this tidbit with me.

5. Based in part on information in *Here Comes the Sun*, Gayle Rosellini and Mark Worden (Center City, Minn.: Hazelden Educational Materials, 1987).

6. Lonny Owen is a C.A.C. facilitator with eight years experience counseling codependents and families.

7. This came from Lonny Owen.

8. Based in part on "Relapse Warning Signs for Co-Alcoholism," developed by Terence T. Gorski and Merlene Miller, from "Co-Alcoholic Relapse," in *Co-dependency, An Emerging Issue*, 82.

SECTION III

HISTORY AND
CURRENT EVENTS

We go back . . . and back . . . and back . . .
until we discover the exuberant, unencumbered, delightful
and
lovable child that was, and still is, in us.
And once we find it, we love and cherish it,
and never, never let it go.

CHAPTER 8

"Does anyone need anything more from the group?" the therapist asked. "Yes," replied a woman. "Could you all come with me to a family reunion this weekend so I don't lose my mind?"

Coming to Terms with Our Family of Origin

For years, I thought about doing family of origin work. For years, I didn't do it. The idea brought several images to mind. I envisioned a patient lying on a psychiatrist's couch, endlessly reminiscing about childhood. I pictured thousand-page family genealogy books.

I tried to do the Transactional Analysis version: Draw three circles for each family member. Stack the circles vertically (like a stick figure of a snowman), then run arrows from each person's circles to another's. Along the arrows, write the psychological messages received from that circle. To find these messages, answer a questionnaire. "Mom always . . . (fill in the blank). Dad usually . . . (fill in the blank). The front of my sweatshirt says . . . The back of my sweatshirt says . . ."

Well, Mom always did different things. Dad usually did too. I was always worried I'd write the wrong answer, so I usually didn't fill in anything. And I didn't own a sweatshirt until I was thirty-three years old, when I bought one at a garage sale. The front of it read, "St. Cloud State University." The back of it was blank, except for a small hole.

With due respect to Sigmund Freud, family trees, and Transactional Analysis, I considered family of origin work expensive, boring, and complicated. The past is over and done with, I thought. Just forget about it. Besides, how could *that* be affecting me *now?* I've since changed my mind. My question has become: How could that *not* be affecting me now?

For many years, therapists have understood the value of doing historical work. They understood its profound influence on current events. Yesterday's smoldering coals — the unresolved feelings and unexamined messages — create today's fires. We work it out, or live it out. What we deny from yesterday, we'll be blind to today. And we'll have many opportunities to deny it because we'll continue to recreate it. Unfinished business may be buried, but it is alive and breathing. And it may have control of our lives.

In recent years, family of origin work has emerged as a significant part of recovery from codependency and the adult child syndrome. Doing our historical work is recognized as one way we can stop allowing ourselves to be affected by other people and their issues.

Many methods for doing historical work have emerged too.

"Moving Through Unfinished Business"

Bedford Combs, founding president of the South Carolina Association for Children of Alcoholics, uses an experiential process in his workshop, "Moving Through Unfinished Business: The Recovery Journey from Codependency."

In a gentle voice, Combs encourages us to get comfortable. Then he plays *The Rose* on a cassette recorder:

Some say love it is a river . . .
When the night has been too lonely . . .

When the room feels safe, Combs talks about families. He talks about control-release systems, where periods of controlling are balanced by times of acting out or releasing. He talks about other families, where times of self-care and nurturing are balanced by periods of creativity and experimentation.

Then Combs draws a picture of our memory center on the blackboard. Maybe we had an alcoholic parent, he said. And to survive, we had to take care of that parent as well as other people in our family. We couldn't be a child, and that hurt. Instead of feeling the hurt, we froze it. He draws a frozen nugget of pain in the memory center. Maybe someone abused us and we froze that pain. Maybe we were so angry at our parents we thought we hated them. And we felt guilty about feeling that way, so we froze that.

Combs talks about overwhelming feelings, feelings that hurt too much to feel. He talks about different coping behaviors we use to stop the pain. He says it was okay we did those things; protecting ourselves helped us survive. But he also says those frozen feelings and coping behaviors may now be blocking us from ourselves and others. He talks about people who have the courage to face those feelings. The reward is great, he says, because the scars from the pain turn into an ability to love and be loved.

He talks about family of origin work — experiential style.

Other Methods of Dealing with the Past

Earnie Larsen, a recovery professional, has developed another method for doing family of origin work. What undesirable consequence are we experiencing today? What behavior are we doing to create that consequence? What's the rule or message from the past that generates the behavior?[1]

Some people use a family geneagram to do historical work.[2] A geneagram is a family tree drawn with little square boxes, one for each family member. Squares on the top line represent grandparents. Underneath, we draw squares representing Mom and Dad. On the next line, we draw squares for ourselves, our brothers and sisters. We include any significant people, such as Great Aunt Helen, the woman who really raised Father.

After we put each person's name in a box, we add descriptive phrases. The phrases can characterize the person, how we felt about or around a person, or what others said about him or her. We don't have to wring our subconscious or our hands to do this. We write whatever comes to mind, and we keep it simple. If we remember Grandpa was scary, mean, laughed a lot, or never noticed us, we write it down. If we remember double messages — Grandpa said he was glad to see us but ignored us for the rest of the visit — we write both. We mention addictions and other problems. For example, we might write that Dad drank a lot, worked all the time, couldn't hold a job, never worked up to his potential, gambled, was overweight, or had affairs.

We write the "bad" and the "good." We mention family roles. Role descriptions describe how people got their attention. For instance, sister Mabel got all her attention by taking care of people; acting naughty; or being smart, cute, or funny. Or, nobody noticed sister Mabel. She didn't get any attention.

We describe our relationships with the people. Maybe a relationship was characterized by someone neglecting us while we waited, hoping someday to be noticed. Maybe someone tried to control us, and we rebelled. Maybe we turned ourselves inside out to get approval from someone who never gave us approval. Maybe we had to play an inappropriate role with a parent.

"My mother never had a fulfilling relationship with my father or anyone else," recalls one man, a recovering adult child of an alcoholic. "She looked to me to meet her needs: her need to be close, to share feelings, to go places with. She never touched me sexually, not once, but it was an incestuous relationship. I wasn't her child," he says, "I was her husband."

We draw a picture of our family, using boxes and words. We remember, and say, what happened. We do this without guilt, because it's okay to talk about things now. Writing it down is important; we gain insights from writing we can't from contemplation.

These are only three of many possible approaches to family

of origin work. Some counselors specialize in family of origin work. We can use the Transactional Analysis version. Or we can use the Fourth and Fifth Steps of Twelve Step programs.

Some of us do historical work when we begin recovery. Some of us aren't ready for a while. Some of us tackle the entire business in one clump; others of us string it out, doing it naturally and gradually as issues and insights surface.

However and whenever we do it, we don't do it to blame or disrespect our families. Nor is the purpose to stay entrenched in yesterday's muck. The goal is to forget the past — after we *remember* what happened. The goal is to become free of its destructive or self-defeating influences.

In the following pages we'll discuss the elements that can help us break free of the past. These include

- feelings
- messages
- patterns
- people

Feelings

One part of historical work is feeling and releasing frozen, denied feelings. I'm a controlling person. I've spent many years trying to make people be who they weren't and do things they didn't want to. I've also tried to control my feelings by willing them away. One way I've done this is by going numb, freezing feelings. In my freezer of feelings, I have a full shelf from childhood. I didn't deal with feelings then, but they didn't go away. They're in storage. Some are big; some are little. Some have been stored so long they have freezer burn. They're stored in body tissue, in messages, and behaviors.

Remembering events is one way to expose these feelings. We recall an event, then follow it to an emotional conclusion. What was the feeling we had during or after an event? Did we feel it or freeze it? How we felt about an experience — rather, *what we didn't feel but needed to* — is as important as what happened. We're safe now. We let ourselves feel the fear, shame, rage, hurt, and loneliness we didn't feel safe enough to feel then. We may even want to play with fantasy, to go back and pretend we had better ways to protect ourselves. We're ten feet tall; we've got a shield and a sword; we have whatever we need to protect ourselves. Then we come back to reality. We know we're grown up now and can take care of ourselves.[3]

This work isn't to be done casually. Many of us have frozen big wounds. If we open them, we need to know we're doing it with someone who can help us properly close the incisions. A good rule of thumb is: If you can't close it, don't open it. Some people find complete blocks to the past. Denial is a necessary safety device.[4] We use it to protect ourselves. If that protective device is taken from us, we need other protection.

Not having any recollection of certain times in our lives may be a key to historical work. Or, repeatedly thinking or talking about certain past events can indicate unfinished business. Resolving it will help dissolve it. Unfinished business remains in the air, in us, and in our lives. We will be attracted, drawn, compelled to what is unfinished in us. Experiencing and releasing the feelings completes the transaction.

"These feelings can be overwhelming and scary," says therapist Scott Egleston, who works with juveniles. "Some of the kids in my program tell me they're afraid they'll disappear if they feel all that pain."

The child in us may fear the same thing. Don't worry. We won't disappear. Once we feel and release those emotions, we'll appear.

Messages

Another important goal of family of origin work is decoding and changing the self-defeating messages we picked up as children. The message is the meaning we interpreted from what happened. It's our frame of reference — our filing catalog for life's events.[5] Our messages may be related to the codependent rules:

- It's not okay for me to feel.
- It's not okay for me to have problems.
- It's not okay for me to have fun.
- I'm not lovable.
- I'm not good enough.
- If people feel bad or act crazy, it's my fault.

"When we're young, we don't have the experienced frame of reference adults have to make sense of things," Egleston says. "When someone, especially someone we love, behaves inappropriately or treats us badly, we don't see the behavior connected to a person's problem or addiction. We don't understand that it's *their* issue. Our only frame of reference is, 'It must be me. There must be something wrong with me.' "

We each have our own set of messages unique to our circumstances and to us. Each person can interpret entirely different messages from the same event.[6]

Messages control, or generate, our behaviors. Some messages are good and allow us to do certain things without thinking too much about them: "Be a good student." "Pay your bills on time." "Don't get into the car with strangers." Other messages may be neutral: "Go to your room if you're going to cry." It can be interesting to decode these messages, but we don't need to be overly concerned with them. It's the destructive ones, the "It's not okay to be who I am" or "I'm not lovable" messages we want to change. Those generate self-defeating behaviors.

One way to understand our messages is to use Earnie Larsen's approach:

- What is today's undesirable consequence?
- What behavior is causing the consequence?
- What's the rule (yesterday's message) that generates the behavior?

"One consequence was that I never had any money, no

matter how much I earned," says one man. "I used Larsen's formula. The behavior was that I spent money the second I got it. The rule or message was that I wasn't financially responsible; I didn't know the value of a dollar, and I didn't deserve to have money."

Another way to uncover our messages is to start listening to ourselves. If we listen closely, with an ear toward understanding, we'll hear the message. It's right there, under the behavior.

Once we've decoded our messages, we give ourselves new, more constructive ones. It's a big job, but so are the rewards from doing it.

Patterns

Another goal of historical work is to understand and change self-defeating patterns, including our patterns of intimacy or intimacy avoidance. What keeps happening, over and over? What do I keep doing, over and over? What do other people keep doing to me, over and over? Why do I need this to happen? How and why do I attract it? How do the characteristics of today's relationships connect to my past relationships?

"I continually found myself in relationships with men who said they loved me, but they couldn't show that love or be close to me because they were addicted," says one woman. "My idea of intimacy was me waiting endlessly for something that wasn't going to happen. Then I realized this was the same pattern I had, and still have, with my brother and father."

"The men in my family were sex addicts," says another woman. "I spent my childhood feeling scared and uncomfortable around men, and wondering what was wrong with me for feeling that way. Then I went on to create the same patterns in my adult life."

"As a child, I was surrounded by very negative, controlling people. Guess what kind of people I attracted when I grew up? The same," reported a third woman.

Some of us may have more than one pattern. "I find myself alternating patterns. In one relationship, I create my pattern with my father; in the next, my pattern with my mother," explains a fourth woman.

We also examine our roles. How did we get our attention as children? How do we get our attention today?

The feelings, messages, patterns, and roles are connected, interwoven like a tapestry.

People

An important part of family of origin work is resolving our relationships with the people in our families. This means acknowledging and releasing any intense feelings about family members, so we are free to love and grow. That can mean running a gamut of emotions from denial, hate, rage, disappointment, frustration, rejection, disillusionment, wishful thinking, resentment, and despair to acceptance, forgiveness, and love. Many adult children wish circumstances and people could have been, or would be different. They weren't and aren't. And although our feelings toward family members and our childhoods are valid, these feelings can block our growth if we don't resolve them.

We have our family of origin issues, and so do other family members. Often, our parents have more severe family of origin issues than we do. In recovery, we learn to accept the darker side of ourselves. In family of origin work, we learn to accept the darker side of our parents too.[7]

"We forget our parents were people before and after they became parents," says Egleston.

In *You Can Heal Your Life,* one of the best books I've read on self-love, Louise Hay suggests a powerful visualization exercise to help achieve compassion and forgiveness for our parents.

Begin to visualize yourself as a little child of five or six. . . . Now let this little child get very small, until it is just the size to fit into your heart. Put it there so whenever you look down you can see this little face looking up at you and you can give it lots of love.

Now visualize your mother as a little girl of four or five, frightened and looking for love and not knowing where to find it. Reach out your arms and hold this little girl and let her know how much you love her. . . . When she quiets down and begins to feel safe, let her get very small, just the size to fit into your heart. Put her there, with your own little child.

Now imagine your father as a little boy of three or four, frightened, crying, and looking for love. . . .Let him get very small, just the size to fit into your heart. Put him there so those three little children can give each other lots of love and you can love them all.[8]

Besides dealing with our feelings about family members, we learn to function in relationships with them, when possible. Some people have an easy time dealing with family. Others have a difficult time. Some have an awful struggle. For those of us in the last two categories, the solution means practicing self-care and basic recovery principles the best we can, one day at a time. We can't change others, but we can change ourselves. We don't have to take other people's behaviors personally. If they have no love or approval to give us, it isn't our fault. They may not have any to give anyone, including themselves.[9] Some say family of origin work means accepting that one or both of our parents didn't love us. Others, and I agree, say it means accepting our parents couldn't show their love for us in ways we wanted, but loved us the best they could, and maybe more than we thought.

Some people need to take a break from certain family members until they (the recovering people) feel more equipped to deal with these relationships.

"I've really struggled with family relationships," says one woman. "My father molested me for years. My mother knew.

I've tried going home and pretending nothing happened. I've tried getting them to deal with the abuse. They weren't ready. Sometimes, I've needed to stay away. Some people recommended that I stay away forever, but I don't want to," she admits. "They're the only mom and dad I'll ever have. My family is important to me. For years, I used their treatment of me to justify punishing them emotionally and blackmailing them financially. What I'm working on now is trying to forgive them and still take care of myself. I'm working at changing my behaviors with them. I visit them when I feel good, when I want to, and when I can handle it. I'm working at taking responsibility for me."

"My dad is still drinking, and my mom's still a martyr," explains a man recovering from codependency. "For many years I needed to back off from them. Now, I can go home. I can do things with my parents. I can let them be who they are, enjoy what's good, let the rest go, and take care of myself when I need to."

We go back to our families when we're ready. When we go back, we go back differently. We're not part of the system anymore. We have a new system of self-care, self-love, and self-responsibility.

Also, just because we have an insight doesn't mean other family members will be ready to hear or appreciate that insight. In fact, discussing our issues with them may trigger their defenses. We each deal with our secrets and issues when we're ready. The purpose of family of origin work is to benefit us; it's not to change other family members. The best way to help people, including family members, is to keep doing our own work.[10]

The pull and demands of a dysfunctional family are strong. Listen, can you hear the disease singing in the background?[11] Can you understand that diseases like chemical dependency and intergenerational abuse create victims of everyone? Do you know it's not your fault? It's probably not your parents' fault, either. Do you know you have a right to become as healthy as you want, no matter what your family does or doesn't do? Do you know you can love people anyway? Do you know that you're lovable?

Like recovery, family of origin work is a process. It's a healing process, an awareness process, a forgiveness process, and a process of changing and becoming changed. It's a grief process, in which we mourn the things we lost or never had. We deny, get angry, bargain, feel the pain, then finally accept what was and is. After we accept, we forgive. And we take responsibility for *ourselves*. We'll do this when we're ready, when it's time, and when we've worked through the other emotions. When we can do this, the good will shine through if we let it and look for it. The process starts with willingness.

We go back to the house we grew up in. We walk around to each dark room, turn on the lights, and look around. We expose the secrets, the problems, the addictions, the messages, the patterns, and the feelings. We look at events and people. We look at roles and survival behaviors. We see what we're denying today because we denied it yesterday. We see what needs weren't met yesterday and how we may still be reacting to that deprivation. Then after we've stared at our childhood and felt what we needed to feel, we release our feelings. We let go, so we can appreciate what was and is good. We do this courageously, fearlessly, and with compassion — for others and for ourselves — when we're ready to do this.

We go back long enough to see what happened and how that's affecting us now. We visit yesterday long enough to feel and be healed. We come back to today knowing we're free to make choices. We go to war with the messages, but we make peace with the people because we deserve to be free.

We go back . . . and back . . . and back . . . through the layers of fear, shame, rage, hurt, and negative incantations until we discover the exuberant, unencumbered, delightful, and lovable child that was, and still is, in us.

And once we find it, we love and cherish it, and never, never let it go.

Activity

1. What are some significant events from your past that you find yourself repeatedly thinking or talking about? Have you dealt with your feelings about those events?

2. As a start toward accomplishing family of origin work, you may want to try the family geneagram approach described in this chapter. With a friend or in group, draw a picture of your family, using boxes and words.

3. What are some messages you've uncovered? How have you worked at changing those?

4. When you're ready, write a letter to family members, telling them everything you like and think is good about them. You don't have to mail it, but you can if you want.

ENDNOTES

1. This is an indirect quote taken from Earnie Larsen's Adult Children seminar at Trinity Lutheran Church, Stillwater, Minn., spring, 1988.

2. The geneagram method is a popular one, used by many counselors and family programs across the nation. Most counselors develop their own method of using it. I developed this adaptation with Lonny Owen's help during the ten-week workshop and support group we co-facilitated.

3. Scott Egleston generated the core of these fantasy ideas in one of our conversations about family of origin work. He uses it in his family of origin work with teenagers.

4. Melody Beattie, *Denial* (Center City, Minn.: Hazelden Educational Materials, 1986).

5. Again, this thought emerged from the mind of Scott Egleston during a family of origin conversation.

6. Originally, Jessie Roberts taught me this during Transactional Analysis training in the mid-seventies. It's been around for years, and applies to adult children of alcoholics and dysfunctional families syndrome.

7. Earnie Larsen and other family systems counselors teach this.

8. Louise L. Hay, *You Can Heal Your Life* (Santa Monica, Calif.: Hay House, 1984), 78-79.

9. This is a paraphrase from Earnie Larsen's adult children lectures.

10. This idea was generated by Bedford Combs.

11. This idea was also generated by Combs. In his lecture he says that in his therapy program for codependency issues, he has a chorus of people actually "sing" the disease in the background, to help people recognize dysfunctional messages and patterns.

CHAPTER 9

*"How does one become a butterfly?" she asked
pensively. "You must want to fly so much that you
are willing to give up being a caterpillar."*
— *Trina Paulus*
Hope for the Flowers

Breaking Free

"Eureka! The rules are real! They're a living entity."

That light went on one dark night, while I lay in bed confused by a previously unexplained funk of several months. I'd been recovering from codependency for several years. I'd heard and *taught* about the codependent rules.[1] But in that moment, I finally gave the rules the respect they deserved.

The rules position themselves in our control center. They jam things up and take over. They direct our behaviors, and sometimes our lives. Once situated, they program us to do things that leave us feeling miserable, stuck, and codependent.

That's what happened to me. The rules had crept back in and I hadn't noticed. Actually, I had lived with them so long they felt comfortable. But I felt crazy because I was doing what they instructed:

- Don't feel or talk about feelings.
- Don't think, figure things out, or make decisions — you probably don't know what you want or what's best for you.
- Don't identify, mention, or solve problems — it's not okay to have them.
- Be good, right, perfect, and strong.
- Don't be who you are because that's not good enough.

- Don't be selfish, put yourself first, say what you want and need, say no, set boundaries, or take care of yourself — always take care of others and never hurt their feelings or make them angry.
- Don't have fun, be silly or enjoy life — it costs money, makes noise and isn't necessary.
- Don't trust yourself, your Higher Power, the process of life or certain people — instead put your faith in untrustworthy people; then act surprised when they let you down.
- Don't be open, honest, and direct — hint, manipulate, get others to talk for you, guess what they want and need and expect them to do the same for you.
- Don't get close to people — it isn't safe.
- Don't disrupt the system by growing or changing.[2]

People don't make these rules. Addictions, secrets, and other crazy systems make these rules to protect the addictions and secrets and keep the crazy systems in place. But people follow these rules. And people mindlessly pass them on from generation to generation. The rules are the guardians and protectors of the system — the crazy system.

Many of us have lived with and learned these rules. Experts like lecturer Robert Subby say that above all else, even beyond living with a drinking alcoholic, these rules are the tie that binds most of us together in this trap called codependency.[3] Following these rules keeps us locked into codependency; breaking them is a key to recovery.

When you were a child, what happened when you felt sad, angry, or frightened? What happened when you told someone about your feelings? Were you criticized, ignored, told "Hush" or "Don't feel that way"? How did family members deal with feelings? Were you allowed to make decisions? What did others say about your choices? What happened when you pointed out a problem? Were you told you could solve your problems? Were things explained in a way that made sense? Was denial a way of life? Was conflict allowed, then resolved?

Did you know it was okay to be who you are, and that you're good enough? Did anybody teach you how to take care of yourself? Did you have fun? Did people in your family enjoy life? Were you encouraged to trust yourself, God, and life?

Did people in your family talk openly, honestly, and directly? Or was the air thick with tension while people smiled and said, "Fine"? Did you learn how to be close to people? What happened when you tried to grow, change, or step outside the system? Did someone in the family agitate, complain, develop a problem or crisis, or otherwise make such a loud noise you came back? What happens in your family now?

Some, all, or variations of the rules may be operating. We may have more rules than these. Since hearing author Bedford Combs lecture on "lookin' good" families — families that look good but feel crazy because feelings and problems aren't allowed — I've added another possible rule: Always *look* good, no matter how you feel or what you have to do.

We may have been taught directly or indirectly to follow these rules. Powerful methods such as shame, disapproving looks, or role modeling may have enforced them. Once we learn the rules, they govern silently but surely. We begin to feel a feeling. The "don't feel" rule gets triggered. We automatically stop the process of feeling. We decide to do something special for ourselves. The idea or act triggers the "don't be selfish" mandate.

Thinking about or doing a behavior that violates the rules may trigger the rule. Being around a person or system that follows the rules can also activate our rules. Once the rules become our messages, they operate unbidden. They keep us "in line" by dishing out negative consequences of guilt, shame, and fear if we break them without consciously giving ourselves permission to do that.

"An old friend, a recovering alcoholic, called me to borrow

money," recalls Sandy, who's recovering from codependency. "Something didn't feel right about it, but when I thought about saying no, I felt waves of guilt and shame. How could I be so selfish? I loaned him the money, and two weeks later learned he'd been drinking again — for over a month. Now I can clearly see how the message 'don't be selfish' clicked in and kept me from doing what I wanted. I'm trying to learn to recognize the messages when they pop up, instead of two weeks later."

Many of us are attracted to and feel comfortable around people and systems with rules similar to ours.[4] If the system or person has different rules, we'll catch on soon. Rules are powerful, quick to make themselves known.

It's Okay to Change the Rules

Over time, in recovery, we make new rules. Gradually, we learn — from people in our support groups, counselors, healthy friends, and recovery literature and tapes — that it's okay to break the rules. But if we try to change our behaviors without changing the rules, we may find ourselves in conflict with our control center.

Instead of being in conflict or waiting for time and happenstance to give us new rules, why not consciously change the rules? Like the other coping behaviors we *used* to use, the rules were only valuable as a protective device when we had no other way to protect ourselves. We had to get along and survive then. We can choose now.

When I first began detaching from the alcoholics in my life, when I made a conscious choice to give other people's lives back to them and reclaim my own, I had such a puny sense of self that I felt like a deflated balloon. Living in close proximity to active alcoholism contributed to that. My active codependency contributed to that. But following the rules for over thirty years contributed to it all — my weak sense of self, living in close proximity to alcoholics, and my codependency. The rules don't allow for *self*. The rules didn't let me be a healthy person. They didn't allow me to be, much less be me.

The rules strip us of our God-given personal power — our human, mental, emotional, physical, and spiritual rights. We don't have to forfeit our personal power to these messages. We can give ourselves new rules once we've accepted — surrendered to — the old ones. Surrender usually precedes empowerment. (In my life, surrender usually precedes everything.) And how much we're willing to surrender is usually how much we'll be empowered.

Here's our first new rule: It's okay to change the rules. We have the power, the ability, and the right. Whether we've been recovering for ten minutes or ten years, it's never too early or too late to assertively — even aggressively — change the rules. We can take back our personal power. We'll be empowered. And when we change the rules, our behaviors will change.

My new rules are:

- It's okay to feel my feelings and talk about them when it's safe and appropriate, and I want to.
- I can think, make good decisions, and figure things out.
- I can have, talk about, and solve my problems.
- It's okay for me to be who I am.
- I can make mistakes, be imperfect, sometimes be weak, sometimes be not so good, sometimes be better, and occasionally be great.
- It's okay to be selfish sometimes, put myself first sometimes, and say what I want and need.
- It's okay to give to others, but it's okay to keep some for myself too.
- It's okay for me to take care of me. I can say no and set boundaries.
- It's okay to have fun, be silly sometimes, and enjoy life.
- I can make good decisions about who to trust. I can trust myself. I can trust God, even when it looks like I can't.
- I can be appropriately vulnerable.

- I can be direct and honest.
- It's okay for me to be close to some people.
- I can grow and change, even if that means rocking a bunch of boats.
- I can grow at my own pace.
- I can love and be loved. And I can love me, because I'm lovable. And I'm good enough.

We've lived with the old rules for a long time. Breaking them and following new messages may not feel comfortable at first. That's okay. We can do it anyway. As I said earlier, the old rules probably weren't pasted on the refrigerator, but they might as well have been. If we've been following them all our lives, they're glued in our minds. It may take more than once, twice, or a hundred times to make the new rules stick. And we may want to paste the new ones on the refrigerator.

We can think. We can feel. We can figure things out. We can solve our problems and let go of those we can't solve. We can stop taking care of other people and start taking care of ourselves. We can enjoy life. We can be close, trust, grow, change, and love. It's okay to do all those things. And it's our responsibility to give ourselves permission.

If we're in a relationship with someone who follows the old rules, that person may react when we break the rules. He or she may feel all the feelings we feel when a rule tries to enforce itself: fear, guilt, shame, and anxiety. He or she may want us to feel that way too. But we don't have to feel that way. If we do feel that way, we don't have to let our feelings stop us. Living by new messages, we can gently but powerfully give people around us permission to live by new rules.

Break free by surrendering. Break free by breaking the rules. Work at enforcing new rules. Work at them until they become as powerful and alive as the old rules. Work at them until you've reclaimed yourself and your life. Then work at them some more.

When you get stuck, when the old stuff comes back, when people tell you "you shouldn't," when you start to wonder if they're right, redouble your efforts. When the guilt and fear and shame come rushing in, pound the new rule into your conscious mind. Ask your Higher Power to help. Surround yourself with people who'll support you in your efforts, people striving to live by new rules. Support them in their efforts too. It's called recovery.

Rules are rules, but some rules are made to be broken.

Activity

1. What are your old rules? What new rules do you want to start living by? Write down the rules you want to break, then draw a line through them. Cross them out. Now, write down the new rules of your choosing.

2. Learn to recognize when an old message is trying to control your behavior. Pay attention to how you feel. Use those times to consciously affirm your new rule.

3. Visualization work can help us change rules. We know the behaviors the old rules generate; what behaviors will the new ones generate? Imagine what it would look like following the new rules. What, specifically, will you do differently when you're following a new rule? What will that look like? Feel like? Sound like?

ENDNOTES

1. The codependent rules I refer to throughout this book are based on Robert Subby and John Friel's work in "Co-Dependency — A Paradoxical Dependency," in *Co-Dependency, An Emerging Issue* (Pompano Beach, Fla.: Health Communications, Inc., 1984), 34-44.

2. Ibid.

3. Robert Subby, "Inside the Chemically Dependent Marriage: Denial & Manipulation," in *Co-Dependency, An Emerging Issue*, 26.

4. Ibid., 27.

CHAPTER 10

I'm pore, I'm black, I may be ugly and can't cook, a voice say to everything listening. But I'm here.
— *Celie, from* The Color Purple,
by Alice Walker

Breaking Through the Shame Barrier

"You don't have to be ashamed about wanting to be in a relationship," I told the audience. "If you were unemployed, you wouldn't feel ashamed about looking for a job, would you?"

"I would," mumbled a man in the fifth row.

"I went to a dance," said Marcie, a thirty-four-year-old woman recovering from adult children and incest issues. "All I could do was hang my head and stare at my feet."

"You don't ever have to apologize for being who you are. And you don't have to be ashamed of who you are," I told her.

"Well," she replied hesitantly, "maybe sometimes I do."

"I've been recovering from codependency and chemical dependency for years," said one woman. "For many of those years, my sponsor told me she's never seen such a discrepancy between a person's potential, intelligence, and talent and what that person believes about her potential, intelligence, and talent. I'm finally beginning to see what she means. I've never believed in myself! I've never given myself any credit! It's like keeping a high-performance car idling or in park, then complaining because it won't move forward."

Whether we call it "shame bound," "shame based," or "shame faced,"[1] shame can be a burden and problem for many of us. Shame can hold us back, hold us down, and keep us staring at our feet. We may not understand shame technically. We may not be able to label it. We may call it other things: fear, confusion, guilt, rage, indifference, or the other person's fault.[2] But if we're recovering from codependency or adult children issues, we've probably been profoundly influenced by shame.

Shame is the trademark of dysfunctional families. It comes with addictive families, where one or more people were addicted to alcohol, drugs, food, work, sex, religion, or gambling. It comes with families with problems and secrets. It comes with families whose parents, grandparents, or even great-grandparents had addictions, problems, or secrets.[3] Shame adds fuel to the addictive fire. It's used to protect secrets and keep them in place. It's used to keep us in place. And often it's passed from generation to generation, like a fine piece of porcelain, until it rests on the mantle in our living room.

Shame on you. The words are a curse, a spell others cast on us. It's a spell we learn to cast on ourselves. The creepy, crawling muck drips like black ink from our heads to our toes. Whether the spell is cast with a look, certain words, a tone of voice, or an old message inside our heads, it's there until we do something about it. The spell says, "What you did isn't okay, who you are isn't okay, and nothing you do will change that." *Shame on you.*

Shame has its roots in our childhood and its branches in our lives today. Shame is a form of control, a tool used by parents and societies probably since the beginning of time. Shame is the feeling we get when we do something that disappoints people we love. Used properly, it can help instill ethics and a conscience.[4] It is externally-applied guilt.

Appropriate shame tells us certain behaviors are inappropriate, and it separates our behaviors from who we are. "Stop that Johnny!" the mother scolds. "I don't ever want to see you hitting someone again. It's not okay to hit."[5] In this case,

Johnny learns it's not okay to hit, but it's okay to be Johnny. That's not the kind of shame I'm talking about in this chapter. I'm talking about the malignant kind, the shaming that says, "Stop that Johnny. And you're a bad, bad person for doing it in the first place."

In this case, Johnny learns it's not okay to hit, and it's not okay to be Johnny. The externally-applied guilt becomes guilt for being. In some of our families, we are shamed for healthy, appropriate behaviors too, such as thinking, feeling, having fun, loving and being loved, making mistakes, and taking care of ourselves. We may have developed a sense of shame about our bodies, or certain parts of our bodies, or our sexuality.

Sometimes, we become shame based because of what others did to us. Victims of abuse are often plagued by shame, even though they weren't responsible for the inappropriate behavior.

How Shame Can Control Us, If We Let It

For many of us, shame expands from being the feeling we get when we disappoint someone we love to a feeling we get when we provoke anyone's disapproval, even a stranger's disapproval.

"My children were in a restaurant lobby playing with some other children they didn't know. They got into some kid stuff together — making faces at each other, sticking their tongues out," says one recovering woman. "Then the other children's mother got involved. I told her I didn't want to get involved with the children's argument; I had learned both sides usually played a part. She started harping about how bad my kids were, and no wonder because I was a bad mother. I froze. I folded up and died inside. It took me half a day to work through the shame. I let a total stranger put it on me!"

People can control us through our areas of shame. That's what shame is — a tool for controlling behavior. Being vulnerable to shame makes us vulnerable to being controlled.

The thought of people disapproving of us — *casting the spell* — can become enough to stop us. Shame can almost paralyze us.

"Shame binds and blocks the flow of energy," says therapist Scott Egleston.

Let me give an example. Some time ago, I had a problem being late for church. For many reasons, mostly because I was leaving home late, I was arriving late at church. And I began to feel ashamed. What were others thinking of me? What kind of person was I, if I couldn't get myself and the children to church on time? And if I didn't care enough to be on time, why was I even bothering to come at all? I began sneaking into a back pew, berating myself during the entire service instead of listening. Nobody was disapproving of me. I was doing it to myself.

The more ashamed I became, the more I vowed to be on time and the later I was each Sunday. One week, everything went wrong from the time I got up to the time the children and I got to the church sanctuary. Nobody could find the right clothes. Someone spilled their cereal. We were arguing. I felt frantic, and my feelings were spilling over on the entire family. The issue wasn't that it was preferable to arrive on time. The issue had become I wasn't okay if I got to church late. We arrived almost fifteen minutes late.

I stood in the foyer outside the sanctuary. *What an awful person I am*, I thought. *How dare I walk in this late!* Nobody paid any particular attention to me, but I could just see the entire congregation turning to look at me, judging and frowning.

I couldn't walk into the sanctuary. I couldn't move my feet forward. I was paralyzed by shame. I grabbed the children, and whisked them out the door vowing it would never happen again.

The next week I got up, left the house early, and got to church five minutes early. Everybody was getting into their cars and leaving. The service was over. We had gone on daylight savings time that day, and I didn't set the clock forward. I was almost an hour late. I surrendered, and the issue has since become manageable.

The point of the story is this: Shame can stop us from acting. If we grew up in a system that attached shame to healthy behaviors like thinking, feeling, and taking care of ourselves, shame may be stopping us from doing those things. Each time we have a feeling, a thought, have some fun, get close, or just let go with some spontaneous "being," shame can spoil it. Shame can stop us from setting boundaries. And shame can keep us entrenched in our mistakes.

"I became involved with some inappropriate sexual behaviors," recalls one man. "I fell into a situation, and did some things I didn't feel good about at all. Later, I felt so guilty and ashamed. I felt like trash. I didn't know how to deal with all those awful feelings. I didn't know how to forgive and accept myself. The only thing that promised to make me feel better was to do the same thing again. I started a compulsive behavior that went on for several months, until I finally surrendered and forgave myself. I couldn't change the behavior when I hated myself. I could only change when I started loving myself — unconditionally."

Even Opus, the little penguin in the *Bloom County* cartoon strip, had his experience with shame. Some members of the community found Opus reading certain magazines. They charged him with penguin lust, and banished him from the Bloom County kingdom. Hanging his head, the exiled Opus shuffled off to far corners of the world. Sometime later, he accepted employment as a male penguin stripper, the only job he felt worthy of. "I am suffering," Opus said, "from chronically and fatally low self-esteem."

Shame can affect each choice we make: choice of spouse, friends, home, job, or car; how we spend our money; and what we do with our time. Shame can prevent us from seeing our good choices, because we don't believe we deserve the best. If we believe who we are isn't good enough, each encounter with life will prove what we believe, no matter how much good we do. We may seek out or create experiences to reinforce that belief. Sometimes, it will cause us to destroy what's good.

One recovering man tells the following story. "I always wanted a Mercedes," he says. "One day, I bought one. I ordered the car, picked it up, and immediately the worst feeling flooded through me. Whenever I went someplace, I parked a block or two away. I didn't tell anybody I got the car. I felt like wearing a paper bag over my head when I drove it. I didn't know what was wrong; I just knew I felt uncomfortable about the car. One week later, I took it to another car lot and started to trade it for a car of far less value. I was going to lose money! Then it hit me. What was wrong was shame. I didn't believe I deserved that car.

"I kept the car," the man says. "I'm working on my shame. I'm working at changing what I believe about myself, and my right to have nice things."

Shame can make us feel crazy and do crazy things. It hurts to believe it's not okay to be who we are. To protect ourselves from that pain, we may avoid shame by turning it into other feelings that are safer and easier to handle: rage; indifference; an overwhelming need to control; depression; confusion; flightiness; or an obsession to use our drug of choice, whether that "drug" is alcohol, a pill, food, sex, or money. We may transform shame into blame, numbness, or panic. Or we may deal with it by running away.[6]

We may not understand that shame is causing us or others to do these things. It's confusing to be in a relationship with a shame-based person.[7] We see the running, blaming, or rage, and may not understand why we or the other person is doing these things.

I had a dream one night. I was in an underground prison. Other people were in that prison with me. All my choices had to be made from the people and things in that underground prison. When I awoke, I realized that the prison represented shame and low self-esteem. I also realized the door to that prison wasn't locked; it was open. All I had to do was walk through.

In the following pages I'll discuss some ideas to help you start walking through that door. These points include

- switching from a shame-based system to one of self-love and acceptance,
- exposing shame,
- treating shame like a feeling,
- tracking shame to its roots,
- changing what's needed,
- releasing shame, and
- knowing your rights and your rules.

Switch from a Shame-Based System to One of Self-Love and Acceptance

A shame-based system means we operate from the underlying belief that who we are *and* what we do isn't okay. In recovery, we decide who we are is okay. We love and accept ourselves unconditionally. When we do something that's inappropriate we separate the behavior from our identity. What we did may not be okay, but we're okay. Then we take steps to correct our behavior. This is the basic goal in recovery. It's the essence of Twelve Step programs, and it's what working the Steps can accomplish for us.[8]

This healthy system believes if we're working at recovery and connected to our Higher Power, we have an internal moral code that will send signals when it's violated. This system says we can trust ourselves, recovery, and our Higher Power. And it tells us we're okay if we make mistakes, because that's how we learn and grow.

Expose Shame

Learn to recognize the difference between shame and guilt. Guilt is believing that what we did isn't okay. Authentic guilt is valuable. It's a signal that we've violated our own, or a universal, moral code. It helps keep us honest, healthy, and on track. Shame is worthless. Shame is the belief that whether what we did is okay or not, who we are isn't.[9] Guilt is resolvable. We make amends for what we did, learn from our mistake, and attempt to correct our behavior. Shame isn't resolvable. It leaves us with a sense that all we can do is apologize for our existence, and even that falls short of what's needed.

We may have mild, medium, or severe shame attacks. We may live in a constant state of shame. We can learn to recognize and identify shame: how it feels, the thoughts it produces, and what it makes us do. Do you run, hide, blame, freeze, fly into a rage or try to control? Learn to detect when shame is at the core of these behaviors. Hold a light to shame and call it what it is: a nasty feeling dumped on us to impose rules — usually someone else's rules.

Treat Shame Like a Feeling

Shame is a powerful force. For lack of a better word, let's call it a feeling. When it appears, treat it like any other feeling. Talk about it. At least acknowledge it to yourself. Sometimes, I "Gestalt" my way through shame: I hang my head, cover my face with my hands, and say, "I'm so ashamed." Other times, I simply say, "Yes. That's shame." The basic "dealing with feelings etiquette" applies to shame: it's our feeling and our responsibility. Become aware of it. Then accept it. Shame is like any other feeling: denying it won't make it go away; it'll make it get bigger.

Actually, I don't mind those moments when I feel ashamed. I used to feel that way most of the time. Now, I usually have enough self-esteem and good feelings to notice when shame creeps back in.

Track Shame to Its Roots

Why are you feeling ashamed? Who have you disappointed? Who's rules are you breaking? Someone else's, or your own? Maybe we're doing something that's causing us to feel legitimately guilty. Maybe we're violating our own moral code, and guilt has become intertwined with shame. Sometimes, shame is a clue to something we legitimately need to change, but we probably won't change until we get rid of the shame.

Sometimes, shame creeps in about our pasts — something that can't be changed.

Other times, shame indicates we've broken a family rule. We each have our own messages, and shame will be bonded to the messages. Dealing with shame can help us understand our messages. One woman shared the following experience with me.

"Whenever I talked to men, I became flooded with shame," she says. "It didn't matter if it was men friends or a man I was interested in dating. Then, I realized what was happening. When I was an adolescent, my family had some real taboos about being sexual. Whenever my father caught me talking to a boy, he shamed me. The words he used were, 'You ought'a be ashamed. You're acting just like a tramp.'

"I was thirty-five years old, I lived in a different city than my father, but his words were still in my head. The shame was still inside me, each time I talked to a man. Understanding this helped. I've been able to give myself new messages, and the shame is disappearing."

"I felt ashamed each time I left the house without the children," explains another woman, a mother of three children. "Once I stopped running from my shame, I uncovered the message: A good mother always puts her children first. Once I uncovered it, I could change it. My new message is: A good mother takes care of herself too."

Change What's Needed

If we feel ashamed because we've done something we feel guilty about, we convert shame to guilt, then make any appropriate amends and change our behavior. If we decide shame is trying to enforce an unhealthy, inappropriate message on us, we change the message. If we feel ashamed about something we cannot or need not change, we surrender to the situation and give ourselves a big hug.

Release Shame

Once we accept shame's presence, find a way to make it disappear. Talk back to it. Get mad at it. Tell it to go away. Feel it intensely. Make friends with it. Let it go. Work Step Six and Step Seven of the Twelve Step program. Work Step Six by getting ready to have the shortcoming of shame removed, and work Step Seven by asking God to remove it.[10] Handle it however it works for you, but continue with the course of action you choose, and let go of the shame feeling.

Know Your Rights and Your Rules

Many of us grew up with shame bonded to basic human rights and needs.[11] It helps to know our rights and our new rules. Then, we can deal with the shame when it tries to enforce the old rules. We have the right to say no or yes, be healthy, feel safe, and take care of ourselves. We have the right to set limits, be free from abuse, grow at our pace, make mistakes, have fun, and love and be loved. We have the right to our perceptions, observations, opinions, and feelings. We have the right to become as healthy and successful as we can.

We have other rights too. I discovered them the day I discovered my shame "base." I was driving to an appointment I had at a local college with a vocational counselor. I didn't have to take a test. I didn't have to pass an exam. I had nothing to win or lose. I just needed to gather a few pamphlets and get some information. Yet I felt anxious and frightened, which was the way I usually felt. Then I realized what was going on. I felt anxious most of the time because I didn't feel appropriate to life. The situation or circumstance didn't matter. I didn't feel good enough. I wasn't enough.

I made a decision that day. I was here, I was me, and I was

enough in spite of my past, my present, my future, my weaknesses, my foibles, my mistakes, and my humanness.

We're good, and we're good enough. Sometimes we make big mistakes; sometimes we make little mistakes. But the mistake is what we do, not who we are. We have a right to be, to be here, and be who we are. If we're not certain who we are, we have a right to make that exciting discovery. And we don't ever have to let shame tell us any differently.

Activity

1. As you go through your daily activities, keep a record of your shame attacks. Then, look for patterns. In what areas are you most vulnerable to shame: Talking about feelings? Your body? Fun activities? Making mistakes and being imperfect? Your past? Which people seem most prone to trigger your shame?

ENDNOTES

1. This phrase is borrowed from the pamphlet *Shame Faced: The Road to Recovery*, by Stephanie E. (Center City, Minn.: Hazelden Educational Materials, 1986).

2. Ibid., p. 1.

3. Merle A. Fossum and Marilyn J. Mason, *Facing Shame — Families in Recovery* (New York: W. W. Norton & Company, Inc., 1986), 44.

4. This idea, and many in this chapter, came to me from Scott Egleston.

5. This example came from Scott Egleston.

6. Stephanie E., *Shame Faced*, 1.

7. Fossum and Mason, *Facing Shame*, 29.

8. This idea came from Lonny Owen during the workshop we co-facilitated.

9. This definition is fairly common, but I got it from Scott Egleston.

10. Based on Step Six and Step Seven of the Al-Anon Twelve Step program.

11. From Lonny Owen.

CHAPTER 11

*I will take a long look at where I am today and be
grateful for my place. It's right for me now, and is
preparing me for the adventure ahead.*
      — *from* Each Day a New Beginning

From Deprived to Deserving

The psychiatrist showed Jason a sketch.[1]"What does this
look like?"

Jason, a middle-aged man with dusty brown hair, said it
looked like a bird.

"Good," said the psychiatrist. He flipped to the next picture. "And this one?"

Jason said it looked like a tree. The doctor nodded, and
showed Jason the next sketch.

"A butterfly."

"And this one?" the doctor asked.

Jason stared. He examined the picture from all angles. "I
don't know what that is," Jason said.

The psychiatrist showed Jason the next sketch and the one
after that. Neither of those reminded Jason of anything either.
After those three sketches, Jason identified the rest of the
pictures in the test.

"Why couldn't I recognize those pictures?" Jason asked,
when the psychiatrist finished.

"It's not surprising that group of sketches didn't make
sense to you," the psychiatrist said. "They represent a father's love. You'd only be able to recognize the pictures if you
had experienced a father's love. The pictures were blank
because that's a blank spot in your development."

Jason started talking. He talked about being the youngest

of nine children born to a farm family during the depression. He rehashed his fifteen-year battle with alcoholism. He mentioned two failed marriages to women who treated him as his father had — coolly and with rejection. He talked about unceasing efforts to do things for people and not feeling appreciated. Toward the end of the session, Jason paused. When he spoke again, he looked and sounded more like a nine-year-old boy than a fifty-year-old man.

"Why didn't he ever hold me on his lap, or hug me, or tell me he thought I was special?" Jason asked. "Why didn't he ever tell me he loved me?"

"Either he wasn't capable of it, or he didn't know how to show love," the psychiatrist said quietly.

Jason stood up. He had tears in his eyes, but a new strength in his face. "You mean it wasn't me?" Jason said. "It wasn't my fault? I'm not unlovable?"

"No," the doctor said. "You're not unlovable. You were just deprived of love."

The Quest for Normal

Many of us were deprived as children. We may have been so deprived of good feelings that we believed life wasn't worth living. We may have been so deprived of love that we believed we weren't worthwhile. We may have been so deprived of protection and consistency that we believed people were untrustworthy. Our parents may have been so wrapped up in their problems and pain, so deprived themselves, they couldn't give us what we needed. We may have been deprived of material items: toys, candy, clothing, food, or a decent home.

Some of us were deprived of childhood.

It's been said that adult children from dysfunctional families don't know what "normal" is. That's because many of us haven't had much of that either.

My quest for normal has been an enormous undertaking. What's fun? What's love? How does it feel and what does it look like? What's a good relationship? How do you form an opinion? What do you do on your day off? How do you buy clothes? How do you make friends? What do you do with them when you get them? What's crazy? What's sane? How do you make yourself feel better when you hurt? What's the good stuff in life? Is there any? How much can I have?

For many of us, life is a big store. This store has two departments: the main floor, holding display after display of good stuff, much of which we can't label because we've never seen it; and the bargain basement, the room with the leftovers and irregulars. The room where we shop.

Listen to the following conversation between two women. One woman is recovering from adult children issues and a marriage to an alcoholic. The other is of fairly normal descent.

"I can't decide whether to break up with my boyfriend or not," says a woman.

"What are his good points?" asks her friend.

"Well, he works every day. He usually does what he says he's going to do. He's kind. And he's never hit me."

"No," says her friend. "You don't understand. What are his good points? The things you listed are givens."

"Oh," says the woman. "I didn't know that."

Which of the two women do you think is the adult child?

Losses are tough. It hurts to have something, then lose it. Deprivation runs deep. It creates blank spots in us.

"I never had a healthy, loving, present father figure," says one recovering woman. "I had an alcoholic father who left home when I was two; and an uninvolved stepfather for two years, when I was a teenager.

"When I grew up, I had several unsuccessful relationships with those same kinds of men: alcoholic or uninvolved. I didn't know there was anything else. If you've never had ice cream and haven't heard much about it, ice cream isn't part of your world. It's not a choice. Well, healthy, loving men weren't part of my world. They weren't a choice.

"One day, on a bus ride across the state, I sat next to an

elderly gentleman. We chatted, and he told me about his wife, and how lonely he felt because it was the first time in years they had traveled separately. He told stories about his children. He recalled most incidents with happiness. He talked about an incident when his son had asked him to do something, and he was too busy to respond. He said he felt guilty about it for years, until one day he mentioned it to his son and his son couldn't even remember.

"What he didn't say that I heard anyway was he was there for his family in some substantive ways. He was present emotionally, physically, mentally, and financially. He cared about them and was healthy enough to show that.

"My eyes opened to something for the first time," she explains. "I didn't know that kind of man — that kind of husband, father, person, or family — existed in real life. For a moment, sadness flooded through me. I had done some grief work before, but how could I grieve something I didn't know I had lost? I felt sad that I hadn't known that kind of fatherly or family love. Then, I put that information into my reality. That kind of love, that kind of man, was out there."

We need to fill in the blank spots. Many things could be options for us:

- healthy love,
- an identity,
- an underlying feeling of safety,
- a norm of feeling good,
- the ability to resolve conflicts,
- good friends,
- fulfilling work,
- enough money, and
- the unconditional love and protection of a Higher Power.

Many of us were deprived as children, but many of us have carried that deprivation into adulthood. Deprivation creates deprived thinking. Deprived thinking perpetuates deprivation.

We can fall into the trap of short supply thinking: there's good stuff out there, but there isn't enough for us. We may become desperate, scrambling to get what we can and holding tightly to it, whether it's what we want or is good for us. We may become resentful and jealous of people who have enough. We may hoard what we have or refuse to enjoy it, fearing we'll use it up. We may give up and settle for less. Deprivation becomes habitual. We may continue to feel afraid and deprived, even when we're not.

"I buy fifty-two rolls of toilet paper at a time," says one woman, an adult child of an alcoholic who's been married to two alcoholics. "I buy fifty-two rolls of toilet paper at a time because for many years there wasn't enough toilet paper or money to buy more. And I don't ever want to run out again. For the past three years, I've earned over $25,000 a year. There's enough money to buy more. But there doesn't feel like there's enough, or like there's going to be enough."

We may react to deprivation in many ways. We may insist life, and the people in our lives, make up for all we never had. That's unfair, and those expectations can wreck what's good today.

Deprived, negative thinking makes things disappear. We're grumbling about the half-empty water glass, so focused on what we don't have that we fail to appreciate the half-full glass of water, the glass itself, or being alive and well enough to drink the water. We become so afraid that we might not get more, or we're so sour about only having half a glass to drink, we may not drink it. We let it sit on the table until it evaporates. Then we have nothing, which is what we thought we had anyway. It's an illusion! We can drink the water if we're thirsty, then go to the tap and get more.

Perhaps the most profound effect of deprivation is we may decide we don't deserve the good things in life. That isn't true, but our belief will make it true. What we believe we deserve, what we really believe deep inside, will be about what we get.

Deprived, negative thinking can prevent us from seeing what's good in our lives today, and it can stop the good stuff from happening. It hurts to be deprived. It hurts to walk through life believing there's not enough. It's painful to believe we're undeserving. So, stop. Now. You can fill in the blanks with "there's enough" and "I deserve." There's enough for you. There's enough for the person next door too. You deserve the best, whatever that means to you.

The Gratitude Principle

Deprived thinking turns good things into less or nothing. Grateful thinking turns things into more.

Many years ago, when I started rebuilding a life shattered by my chemical use, I dreamt of getting married and raising a family. I also dreamt of owning a house, a beautiful home to be our little castle. I wanted some of the things other people had. I wanted "normal," whatever that was.

It looked like I was about to get it. I got married. I got pregnant. I had a baby girl. Now, all I needed was the home. We looked at all sorts of dream homes — big dream homes and in-between dream homes. The home we bought didn't turn out to be one of those, but it was the one we could afford.

It had been used as rental property for fifteen years, had been standing vacant for a year, and was three stories of broken windows and broken wood. Some rooms had ten layers of wallpaper on the walls. Some walls had holes straight through to the outdoors. The floors were covered with bright orange carpeting with large stains on it. And we didn't have money or skills to fix it. We had no money for windows, curtains, paint. We couldn't afford to furnish it. We had three stories of a dilapidated home, with a kitchen table, two chairs, a high chair, a bed, a crib, and two dressers, one of which had broken drawers.

About two weeks after we moved in, a friend stopped by. We stood talking on what would have been the lawn if grass had been growing there. My friend kept repeating how lucky

I was and how nice it was to own your own home. But I didn't feel lucky, and it didn't feel nice. I didn't know anyone else who owned a home like this.

I didn't talk much about how I felt, but each night while my husband and daughter slept, I tiptoed down to the living room, sat on the floor and cried. This became a ritual. When everyone was asleep, I sat in the middle of the floor thinking about everything I hated about the house, crying, and feeling hopeless. I did this for months. However legitimate my reaction may have been, it changed nothing.

A few times, in desperation, I tried to fix up the house, but nothing worked. The day before Thanksgiving I attempted to put some paint on the living and dining room walls. But layers of wallpaper started to peel off the minute I put paint on them. Another time, I ordered expensive wallpaper, trying to have faith I'd have the money to pay for it when it came. I didn't.

Then one evening, when I was sitting in the middle of the floor going through my wailing ritual, a thought occurred to me: *Why don't I try gratitude?*

At first I dismissed the idea. Gratitude was absurd. What could I possibly be grateful for? How could I? And why should I? Then, I decided to try anyway. I had nothing to lose. And I was getting sick of my whining.

I still wasn't certain what to be grateful for, so I decided to be grateful for everything. I didn't feel grateful. I willed it. I forced it. I faked it. I pretended. I made myself think grateful thoughts. When I thought about the layers of peeling wallpaper, I thanked God. I thanked God for each thing I hated about that house. I thanked Him for giving it to me. I thanked Him I was there. I even thanked Him I hated it. Each time I had a negative thought about the house, I countered it with a grateful one.

Maybe this wasn't as logical a reaction as negativity, but it turned out to be more effective. After I practiced gratitude for about three or four months, things started to change.

My attitude changed. I stopped sitting and crying in the

middle of the floor and started to accept the house — as it was. I started taking care of the house as though it were a dream home. I acted as if it were my dream home. I kept it clean, orderly, as nice as could be.

Then, I started thinking. If I took all the old wallpaper off first, maybe the paint would stay on. I pulled up some of the orange carpeting and discovered solid oak floors throughout the house. I went through some boxes I had packed away and found antique lace curtains that fit the windows. I found a community action program that sold decent wallpaper for a dollar a roll. I learned about textured paint, the kind that fills and covers old, cracked walls. I decided if I didn't know how to do the work, I could learn. My mother volunteered to help me with wallpapering. Everything I needed came to me.

Nine months later, I had a beautiful home. Solid oak floors glistened throughout the house. Country-print wallpaper and textured white walls contrasted beautifully with the dark, scrolled woodwork that decorated each room.

Whenever I encountered a problem — half the cupboard doors are missing and I don't have money to hire a carpenter — I willed gratitude. Pretty soon, a solution appeared: tear all the doors off and have an open, country kitchen pantry.

I worked and worked, and I had three floors of beautiful home. It wasn't perfect, but it was mine and I was happy to be there. Proud to be there. Truly grateful to be there. I loved that home.

Soon the house filled up with furniture too. I learned to selectively collect pieces here and there for $5 and $10, cover the flaws with lace doilies, and refinish. I learned how to make something out of almost nothing, instead of nothing out of something.

I have had the opportunity to practice the gratitude principle many times in my recovery. It hasn't failed me. Either I change, my circumstances change, or both change.

"But you don't know how deprived I am!" people say. "You don't know everything I've gone without. You don't know how difficult it is right now. You don't know what it's like to have nothing!"

Yes, I do. And gratitude is the solution. Being grateful for what we have today doesn't mean we have to have that forever. It means we acknowledge that what we have today is what we're supposed to have today. There is enough, we're enough, and all we need will come to us. We don't have to be desperate, fearful, jealous, resentful, or miserly. We don't have to worry about what someone else has; they don't have ours. All we need to do is appreciate and take care of what we have today. The trick is, we need to be grateful first — before we get anything else, not afterward.

Then, we need to believe that we deserve the best life has to offer. If we don't believe that, we need to change what we believe we deserve. Changing our beliefs about what we deserve isn't an overnight process. Whether we're talking about relationships, work, home, or money, this usually happens in increments. We believe we deserve something a little better, then a little better, and so on. We need to start where we're at, changing our beliefs as we're capable. Sometimes things take time.

Believing we deserve good things is as important as gratitude. Practicing gratitude without changing what we believe we deserve may keep us stuck in deprivation.

"I earned $30,000 a year and every morning I got into my ten-year-old car with a busted heater and thanked God for it. I was so grateful," says one woman who's recovering from codependency. "My kids would encourage me to buy a new car and I'd say no; I was just grateful to have my old one. Then one day, when I was talking to someone about deprivation, it hit me that I could afford to have a new car if I really believed I deserved one. I changed my mind about what I deserved, then went out and bought a new car."

There are times in our lives when depriving ourselves helps build character, renders us fit for certain purposes, or is part of "paying our dues" as we stretch toward goals. There is a purpose as well as a beginning and an end to the deprivation. Many of us have carried this too far. Our deprivation is without purpose or end.

In an Andy Capp cartoon strip, Andy's wife came to him one day grumbling about her tattered coat. "That coat of mine is a disgrace. I'm ashamed to go out in it. I'll really have to get a new one," she said.

"We'll see, we'll see," he replied.

"Roughly translated," she said, scrunching up her face, "you never know what you can do without until you try."

Well, we never know what we can have until we try. And we may not know what we already have until we get grateful. Be grateful and believe you deserve the best. You may have more today than you think. And tomorrow might be better than you can imagine.

Activity

1. To help determine what you believe you deserve, complete each of the following statements. Write as many completions as come to your mind for each statement. Write until you ferret out your bottom-line beliefs. Write free-association style, putting down whatever comes to mind. This isn't a test. It's to increase self-awareness. Once you identify any negative beliefs, change them to positive "I deserve" statements. Here is an example of possible answers to the first questions.

I can't or don't have a healthy, loving relationship because:

John wouldn't stop drinking.
There aren't any good men out there.
I don't have time.
It's no use.
Men always leave me.
I give up.
I'll never find love.
I don't know how.
Nobody could love me.

Here's another example:

I can't, or don't have, a job I like because:

I don't have a college degree.
Nobody would hire me.
I don't have a good work history.
I never learned how to do anything.
I'll never amount to anything anyway.
All the good jobs are taken.
I might as well settle for what I've got; it's better than nothing.
Who cares?

Write as many completions to these statements as you can think of.

- I can't, or don't have, a healthy, loving relationship because:
- I can't, or don't have, a job I like because:
- I can't, or don't have, enough money because:
- I can't, or don't have, a comfortable home or apartment because:
- I can't, or don't have, a happy, safe life because:
- I can't, or don't, love myself unconditionally because:
- I can't, or don't have, enough friends because:
- I can't, or don't, have fun because:
- I can't, or don't, accept God's love for me because:
- I can't, or don't, have good health because:
- I can't be successful because:
- I can't be smart enough because:
- I can't be good looking enough because:
- I can't enjoy life because:

ENDNOTES

1. The details about this test, the sketches, and what each sketch resembled, are compiled from Jason's memory and may not be entirely accurate. The crux of the story is.

CHAPTER 12

It's what we all wanted when we were children —
to be loved and accepted exactly as we were then,
not when we got taller or thinner or prettier . . .
and we still want it . . . but we aren't going to get
it from other people until we can get it from
ourselves.

— *Louise Hay[1]*

Affirm Yourself

I used to think affirmations were, well, silly. I have since changed my mind — and my life. I changed my mind because affirmations are a tool that helped change my life. Besides Twelve Step programs and our Higher Power, affirmations may be the most important recovery tool we can embrace.

To "affirm" means to say positively, declare firmly, or assert to be true.[2] In recovery, the concept of using affirmations is closely connected to another term, *empowerment*. To "empower" means to give ability to, enable, or permit.[3]

In the last four chapters we've examined a host of sources for negative messages. Through family of origin messages, living with the "rules," being shamed, and deprivation, many of us have developed a repertoire of negative ideas about ourselves, other people, and life. We may have said, thought, and believed these messages for years. We may have a disciplined ritual for chanting these messages. Many of us have repeated these beliefs so long we've internalized them. The negative messages have become embedded in our subconscious and have manifested themselves in our lives. They've become our premises, our truths, and therefore our reality.

In recovery, we develop a repertoire of positive ideas about ourselves, other people, and life. We develop a disciplined ritual for chanting these messages. We repeat these beliefs so often we internalize them. The positive messages become embedded in our subconscious, and manifest themselves in our lives. They become our premises, our truths, and therefore our reality. That's what affirmations are. We change the energy in ourselves and our lives from negative to positive. Affirmations are how we charge our battery.

Most of us have spent much of our lives asserting and emphasizing certain ideas about ourselves, others, and life. The issue in recovery is choosing what we want to affirm.[4]

"I've done my family of origin work," says one woman. "I know my messages. I know my patterns. But what do I do about it?"

Affirmations and empowerment are "what we do about it." Affirmations are how we change the rules, change the messages, deal with shame, and travel the road from deprived to deserving. We assert new beliefs to be true, give ourselves new permissions, make new messages, and endow ourselves with new abilities. We empower the good and the positive in ourselves and life. Affirmations aren't optional. They are the core of our recovery work. If negative messages have contributed to this havoc, imagine what positive messages can help create!

Affirmations aren't silly little sayings or wishful thinking. They're the antidote to all the negative garbage we've been feeding ourselves for years. Affirmations open the door to good things coming our way, and to the good already there.

The connection between thoughts, feelings, beliefs, physical well-being, and reality has been in the spotlight lately. Books like Louise Hay's *You Can Heal Your Life*[5] and Bernie Siegel's *Love, Medicine & Miracles*[6] have climbed to the top of best-seller charts with good reason. They're making sense. What we think, say, and believe can affect what we do, who we meet, who we marry, how we look, how we feel, the course of our lives, and even, some say, how long we live.[7]

Our beliefs can influence the kinds of diseases and ailments we get, and whether we recover from those ailments.

Affirmations Help Create Reality

Affirmations create space for reality to happen in.[8] The concept of using affirmations in recovery means replacing negative messages with positive ones: we change what we say so we can change what we see. If we emphasize and empower the good in ourselves, we will see and get more of that. If we empower the good in others, we will get more of that too.

The power and responsibility to change our messages and beliefs — to affirm and empower ourselves — lies with each of us. During certain times in our lives we may need to rely on others to empower and affirm us. When I began recovering from codependency, certain people affirmed and empowered me, and it was a gift from God. I try to pass this gift on. I still need people to believe in me and empower me. It's good to do this for each other. But when we begin affirming and empowering ourselves, we'll make giant strides forward.

Recovery is a process, and it's a spiritual one. But aggressively working with affirmations is one of our parts in the process.

To empower means to give power to.[9] What have we been giving power to? The terrible way we look? How bad we feel? Our problems? Another person's problem? Our lack of money, time, or talent? The awfulness of life? Next question: Do we really want to feed and nurture negative ideas — knowing those attitudes will likely create more negative ideas and negative reality? Do we want to empower the problem or the solution?

If our relationships have worked out badly, we may believe that relationships don't work, there aren't any healthy people out there, and people always use us. We may joke about it. We may say it seriously. Or we may keep this thought to ourselves. But it becomes what we believe and expect. If we want to change what happens, we change what we believe and expect. We surrender to what was and is. We let go of our need to have these negative circumstances happen,[10] and we change our behaviors. We accept our present circumstances, but we create space for something different to happen in our lives.

There are good people out there. I am attracted to healthy, loving people, and they to me. A healthy relationship is on its way. We don't obsess about this thought. We don't watch for it to happen. But we may want to think this new thought five times a day or whenever an old, negative thought occurs to us. Then we let go of the results. Whether anything happens today, tomorrow, or next week, we decide this will be our belief. If something contrary to our new belief happens, we don't use the incident to prove our old belief was really true.

We change our family of origin rules and messages from negative to positive. For instance, we change: *I'm not lovable* and *I can't take care of myself* to *I'm lovable* and *I can take care of myself.* We overpower the negative with an equally powerful positive message.

If shame is an issue for us, we might want to focus on the message: *It's okay to be who I am. Who I am is good, and I'm good enough.* We change what we believe we deserve too. From the activity at the end of the last chapter, we can uncover a list of negative ideas begging to be changed to positive assumptions. What we want to affirm is dealer's choice. If we have believed that there are not enough good jobs, good men, money, or love to go around, we start claiming prosperity in those areas.

Our goal in using affirmations isn't to eliminate every negative thought and sad feeling from our lives. That's not healthy nor desirable. We don't want to turn into robots. Feeling sad and angry is sometimes as important as feeling happy and peaceful.

What Affirmations Are and Are Not

Using affirmations doesn't mean we ignore problems. That's denial. We need to identify problems, but we need to empower solutions. Affirmations won't eliminate problems from our lives; affirmations will help solve them.

Affirmations aren't a substitute for accepting reality. They aren't a form of control. They need to be used with heavy doses of surrender, spirituality, and letting go.

Often, it feels awkward and uncomfortable when we start the process of changing negative messages to positive ones. Things may temporarily get worse. Our old ways of thinking surface into conscious awareness. That's good. It's clearing out of our subconscious and making room for the new.[11] A room always looks dirtier when we start to clean it. We pull the unwanted items and trash out of the nooks and crannies. Cleaning intensifies the disorder, until a new order can be created.

It's normal to resist affirmations and positive thoughts. If you've been feeding yourself negative ideas for ten, twenty, or thirty years, of course the positive will feel strange for a while. Give yourself five or ten years of diligently and assertively affirming the good. It won't take that long to manifest itself in your life, but give it time anyway. Be patient. Don't give up. Don't let whatever problems or issues that arise reinforce your old, negative thought patterns.

You'll probably be tested when you turn negative beliefs into positive ones. Often, when I change a belief, a big tidal wave sweeps into my life to try to wash away my new belief. It's as if life is saying, "There! Now what do you *really* believe?" Let the storm roar. Hold fast to your new affirmations. Let them be your anchor. When the storm passes, you'll see you're on solid ground with new beliefs.

Actions That Affirm

Many actions and activities are affirming. In the next pages I've listed some of these.

- Regularly attending Twelve Step support groups and applying those Steps to our lives affirms us and our recoveries.
- Reading meditation books and concentrating on uplifting thoughts is affirming.
- Prayer is an affirmation.
- Listening to audiotapes helps. The self-help audiotape market is rapidly expanding. Subliminal tapes are also becoming popular. On subliminals, only our subconscious hears the affirmations, bypassing any conscious resistance to the positive messages.
- Attending a church we feel comfortable in is an affirmation.
- Attending seminars, workshops, and lectures affirms us.
- The concept of "acting as if" is an affirmation. Another phrase for this concept is "faking it 'til we make it." This doesn't imply a negative use of pretense. It means treating ourselves as if we were already the person we want to become.[12] This is a powerful way to create space for a new reality.
- Written goals are an affirmation.
- Using imagery or visualization is another method for inviting the positive. We create mental images of what we want to happen; we see ourselves as we want to be.
- Positive self-talk is a basic way to affirm ourselves. We force ourselves to think positively. We give ourselves new rules, new messages, and new beliefs. We look in the mirror and talk aloud to ourselves: we look ourselves in the eye and tell ourselves we love us and we're great. It may feel awkward at first, but we'll absorb it as certainly as we absorbed all the negative ideas we've ingested. Looking at old pictures of ourselves and talking positively to those pictures is another helpful technique. We talk positively and lovingly to ourselves at every age and time in our lives. We give ourselves all the good stuff we want and need.

- Written affirmations are helpful too. Many people like to tape positive messages in the bathroom, bedroom, work area, or any place they want a positive focus.
- Surrounding ourselves with friends who believe in us is affirming. What people say, think, and believe about us can have a significant impact on what we believe.
- Affirming others — believing in, supporting, and empowering them — will help us too. If we give some away, we'll have more to keep. Believing in the positive enough to give it away will reinforce and remind us of what we believe.
- Relaxation and fun is affirming.
- Work can be an affirmation of who we are, our abilities, and our creative talents.
- Celebrating our successes and achievements is affirming.
- Giving and receiving compliments is an affirmation.
- Exercise and proper nutrition is an affirmation.
- Therapeutic massage is a form of affirmation that's growing in popularity. Many people recovering from codependency, abuse, and the adult child syndrome have disowned their bodies. Disowning our bodies, splitting from our physical selves, may have been a protective device. To survive physical or emotional pain, we may have frozen our emotions and we may have frozen or numbed our bodies too.[13] The energy supply to certain parts of our bodies may be blocked. Therapeutic massage— nurturing, nonsexual touch—can restore the energy flow and bring needed healing. Our physical selves are as much "us" as our minds, emotions, and spiritual selves.
- Reading positive literature, even watching movies with a positive theme, can be affirming.
- Being grateful is a tremendous way to say yes to the good.
- Hugs help too.
- Love is affirming. Affirmations are love.

The more of our senses we involve with the affirmation process, the more powerful our affirmations will be. Speaking, seeing, hearing, thinking, and positive touch are ways to do this. We inundate ourselves with positive energy. Affirmations are more than little slips of paper we paste to our mirrors — although those slips of paper are important. Affirming ourselves means developing a lifestyle that's self-affirming, instead of self-negating.

Nurturing Ourselves

We develop a way of life that embraces and blends the concepts of self-nurturing and self-discipline. We love ourselves in all the ways we need and deserve to be loved; we discipline ourselves in ways that will be in our own best interests. We become our own best friend and parent.[14]

How do we nurture ourselves? Of all the blank spots we have, this one is often the blankest. If we've never seen, touched, tasted, or felt it, how could we know what nurturing is? Nurturing is an attitude toward ourselves — one of unconditional love and acceptance. I'm talking about loving ourselves so much and so hard the good stuff gets right into the core of us, then spills over into our lives and our relationships. I'm talking about loving ourselves no matter what happens or where we go.

In the morning and throughout our day, we lovingly and gently ask ourselves what we can do for ourselves that would feel good. We ask ourselves what we need to do to take care of ourselves. When we hurt, we ask what would help us feel better.[15] We give ourselves encouragement and support. We tell ourselves we can do it, we can do it good enough, and things will work out. When we make a mistake, we tell ourselves that's okay. We wait a moment, until we get our balance back, and then we ask ourselves if there's something we can learn from our mistake, or if there's some way we can improve our conduct in the future, or if there's an amend we need to make.

We tell ourselves we love and accept ourselves. We tell ourselves we're great and we're special. We tell ourselves we'll always be there for us. We make ourselves feel safe and loved. We do all those wonderful things for ourselves that we wish someone else would have done for us.

If we don't believe we're lovable, why would anyone else? If I don't believe I'm lovable, I can't even believe my Higher Power loves me. If I don't believe I'm lovable, I don't let people, or God, love me. If we love ourselves, we become enabled to love others.

We stop criticizing and lambasting ourselves with harshness. Instead we make a conscious effort to nurture and praise ourselves, because it brings out the best in us.

"I've pushed myself all my life," says Arlene. "If I work hard, I tell myself to work harder. When I get tired, I push myself some more. I do and say all the critical things to myself that my mother did and said to herself and me."

Arlene worried that if she nurtured herself, the work wouldn't get done. She feared if she gave in to her needs, she'd get lazy. She decided to nurture herself anyway, and she was amazed.

"It was my day off. I was exhausted, but I was pushing myself to clean the house. Then I made a decision to nurture myself. I asked myself what would help me feel better, and I decided a nap would. I rested for two hours. When I woke up, I felt like doing the housework. I got it finished, and even had time to go out that night. Nurturing myself didn't make me lazy or ineffective. It made me energized and more effective."

Nurturing is how we empower and energize ourselves. When we love, accept, and nurture ourselves, we can relax enough to do our best. A bonus is, when we love, accept, and nurture ourselves, we're able to do the same for others. We can help them love themselves, and they're more apt to react to us with love and acceptance. It starts a great chain reaction.

Loving and accepting ourselves unconditionally doesn't mean we negate our need to change and grow. It's how we enable ourselves to love and grow.

"Criticism locks us into the very pattern we are trying to change," writes Louise Hay. "Understanding and being gentle with ourselves helps us to move out of it. Remember, you have been criticizing yourself for years and it hasn't worked. Try approving of yourself and see what happens."[16]

There isn't a set of instructions for nurturing ourselves. But if we ask ourselves what would help us feel better or what we need, then listen, we'll hear the answer.

Developing Self-Discipline

Discipline is an individual process. Discipline means we don't always talk about feelings. Sometimes it's not appropriate, or sometimes we need to wait. Discipline means we go through the motions of recovery behaviors on the gray days, the days we're uncertain whether anything is happening or if we're going anywhere on this journey. Discipline means we believe in our Higher Power and His love for us, even when it might not look or feel like He loves us. Discipline means we understand the cause and effect nature of things and choose behaviors that generate the consequences we desire. Discipline is self-control, but not the kind of control many of us have lived with. It's the kind we would teach a child we love very much, because we know that child needs to do certain things in life to live a good life.

When will we become lovable? When will we feel safe? When will we get all the protection, nurturing, and love we so richly deserve? We will get it when we begin giving it to ourselves.

Before I began working with affirmations, my first thought in the morning was "Oh, no. Not another day." It was downhill from there, until I dropped into bed at night, closed my eyes, and said, "Thank God that's over."

Now, when I open my eyes in the morning, I dwell on this thought for a moment: *This is the day the Lord has made. I will rejoice and be glad in it.*[17]

A short time later, I say my morning prayers. While I'm brushing my teeth and putting on my makeup, I tell myself *out loud* that I love myself, I'll be there to take care of myself, God loves me and is taking care of me, I'm good at what I do, and all I need today shall be provided.[18]

During morning break, I read from a meditation book. On my office desk are several cards with uplifting sayings. I have a regular schedule for attending support groups. At least every other day, I talk to a recovering person to give and receive support, encouragement, and acceptance.

Throughout the day, I force-feed positive thoughts into my mind. When I feel ashamed, I tell myself it's okay to be who I am. When I have a feeling, I tell myself it's okay to feel. When I worry about money, I focus on this thought: *My God shall supply all my needs according to His riches in glory.*[19]

I focus on a positive thought whenever a negative, fear-producing thought strikes. I also focus on positive thoughts during those odd moments when I would otherwise be concentrating on negative messages. If I feel panicky or desperate, I ply my mind with positive thoughts. I promise myself I'm safe.

I regularly write goals. I write down what I believe I deserve. I spend an hour a week listening to meditation tapes. I spend a few minutes a week visualizing the good I want to happen. I see what it will look and feel like when it happens. I go in for a therapeutic massage regularly, and work on affirmations during that time. And I will gratitude for almost everything.

This is my regular routine. In times of stress, I intensify efforts. If this sounds like overkill, it isn't. Overkill was all the years I spent focusing on negative, destructive messages.

To discover what you need to work on, spend a day or two listening to your thoughts. Listen to what you say. Listen to the problems and negative qualities you empower in yourself and others. Look in the mirror and notice what you think and say. Sit down to pay bills and listen to your thoughts then. Go to your job and listen to what you think about your work, abilities, and career prospects. Hold your special person in your arms and listen to your thoughts. Listen to how you react to your problems. Listen to what you say to and about your children. What are you giving power to? What are you creating space for? Are you feeding what you want to grow? Change what's needed and make it good. Declare all-out war on your destructive thought patterns.

Many of us have spent years nearly negating ourselves out of existence. Now we're learning to love ourselves into a life of our own.

Activity

1. Spend some time researching your present assertions, beliefs, and premises. Listen to what you say and think. Do this as though you were a detached observer. What do you think and say about yourself, your abilities, your looks, finances, relationships? Is what you're emphasizing what you want to see more of? What problems are you affirming?

2. Write a set of personalized affirmations for yourself. Write loving, empowering affirmations that feel good when you read them. Spend time each day reading these, saying them aloud. You may want to change these as your needs change.

3. Take time, when you're looking in the mirror, to tell yourself you love you, you're beautiful, you're good at what you do. Tell yourself you're going to take care of you, and your Higher Power is caring for you too.

4. Develop a routine of self-care that includes nurturing. You may want to include a daily time for using meditation books, a regular time for attending support groups, a regular program for writing goals, relaxation time, time with friends, and some time for pampering yourself. Choose from any options listed in this chapter, or any others you've discovered. Give yourself the freedom to experiment with different ways of doing this until you find a way that works for you.

ENDNOTES

1. This quote from Louise Hay appeared in an article by Carolyn Rebuen, "Healing Your Life with Louise Hay," *East West* (June 1988), 41.

2. *New World Dictionary of the American Language, Second College Edition* (New York: Simon & Schuster, Inc., 1984), 23.

3. Ibid., 459.

4. This idea grew from Nita Tucker's writing with Debra Feinstein on empowerment in *Beyond Cinderella: How to Find and Marry the Man You Want* (New York: St. Martin's Press, 1987), 155.

5. Louise L. Hay, *You Can Heal Your Life* (Santa Monica, Calif.: Hay House, 1984). Many of the ideas in this chapter were inspired by Hay's work.

6. Bernie S. Siegel, *Love, Medicine & Miracles* (New York: Perennial/Harper & Row, 1986).

7. This idea has been touted by different therapy modalities for years, including Transactional Analysis. Hay and Siegel are saying it again.

8. This idea has been touted for years too. I believe I heard it recently from Louise Hay and from my massage therapist.

9. This idea is from *New World Dictionary of the American Language,* 459, and Nita Tucker's book, *Beyond Cinderella.*

10. This idea based on Hay's writing in *You Can Heal Your Life.*

11. This is based on ideas by Louise Hay in *You Can Heal Your Life* and lectures on the use of affirmations by Earnie Larsen.

12. Based on a quote by Haim Ginott in "Quotable Quotes," *Reader's Digest* (June 1988), cover page.

13. The somatic, or body component, to emotional distress has been explored for a long time by many therapies.

14. This thought was generated years ago by the Rev. Phil Hansen, a pioneer in the chemical addiction recovery movement.

15. This idea based on a suggestion by Louise Hay in *You Can Heal Your Life*.

16. Hay, *You Can Heal Your Life*, 15.

17. Based on Ps 118:24.

18. These ideas inspired by Louise Hay.

19. Based on Phil 4:19.

SECTION IV

RELATIONSHIPS

We accepted powerlessness.
We've found a Higher Power.
We're learning to own our power.
Now we can share the power.

*. . . it is neither cynical nor glib to describe love,
like all of nature, as having its season. Even the
loveliest living things regularly leave for a time . . .
and with equal reliability return.*
— *Martin Blinder, M.D.*[1]

Improving Our Relationships

Relationships are where we take our recovery show on the road. In this section, we'll explore some ideas for improving relationships. Much of the focus will be on special love relationships, but the ideas apply to all our relationships. Many of them can grow into special love relationships too.[2]

Actually, the entire book explores ideas for improving relationships. All our recovery work — dealing with shame, doing our historical work, believing we deserve the best, breaking the rules, learning to affirm and empower ourselves, learning to believe we're lovable — affects our relationships.

There's more to recovery than learning to terminate or avoid relationships. Although some of us may call time-out from certain relationships for a while, recovery isn't done apart from relationships. And relationships aren't done apart from recovery. Recovery is learning to function in relationships.[3] And we learn to function in relationships by participating in relationships.

At a workshop I facilitated, I asked participants how many had failed relationships. Everyone raised both hands. "I didn't know you were going to do jokes," responded one woman.

Many of us have had failed relationships. Many of us are struggling with relationships now. "Kate and I have been married six years," Del says. "We're both from moderately dysfunctional families, and we were both working on recovery years before we married. Sometimes we've worked hard on the relationship. Sometimes we've backed off and worked on ourselves. Sometimes we've been too busy to work on anything. Sometimes we know we really love each other; sometimes it's a real struggle. I never knew relationships were so difficult."

In spite of our struggles, many of us still believe in marriage, family, and love. In spite of our failures, many of us want a loving, committed, fulfilling relationship. We may be afraid and cautious, but, whatever our circumstances, most of us want our relationships to be the best possible. The subject of this chapter, this section, this book, and recovery *is* improving our relationships. The purpose of this chapter is to tell us we can.

Since the beginning of time, people have been struggling to live with, or without, someone they love. Some elements of relationships have changed over the years. We've progressed from a time when people had few choices about choosing a mate, getting a divorce, or living a certain lifestyle, to an age when it's possible to become paralyzed by options. Women have traveled the road from culturally mandated dependency to feminism and a liberation that includes the choice of traditional values. For some people, relationship roles have changed dramatically.

"I don't know what women want or expect anymore," said one man.

"Don't feel bad," I responded. "We're not always sure either."

People are hungry for information about relationships. We want to learn more about how we can make them work, make them work better, and avoid past mistakes. We want to understand and gain insight. In recent years, we've been bombarded with books about relationships. We have relationship enrichment courses, counseling, seminars, and intimacy training. Working on relationships has become one of our many choices about relationships.

"I used to think people just met someone, fell in love, and got married," Hank says. "After recovery, I got into 'a relationship' and discovered I was expected to 'work' on it. I didn't even know what the term meant! Even the word 'relationship' was new to me. We used to call it 'finding a girl friend,' or 'getting married.' "

Nurturing Relationships

We've discovered certain behaviors and attitudes nurture relationships and help them grow. Healthy detachment, honesty, self-love, love for each other, tackling problems, negotiating differences, and being flexible help nurture relationships. We can enhance relationships with acceptance, forgiveness, a sense of humor, an empowering but realistic attitude, open communication, respect, tolerance, patience, and faith in a Higher Power.

- Caring about our own and each other's feelings helps.
- Asking instead of ordering helps.
- Not caring, when caring too much hurts, helps too.
- Being there when we need each other helps.
- Being there for ourselves, and doing our own recovery work helps.
- Having and setting boundaries and respecting other people's boundaries improves relationships.
- Taking care of ourselves — taking responsibility for ourselves — benefits relationships.
- Being interested in others and ourselves helps.
- Believing in ourselves and the other person is beneficial.
- Being vulnerable, and allowing ourselves to get close helps.
- Giving relationships energy, attention, and time helps them grow.

- Initiating relationships with people who are capable of participating in relationships helps.[4]

On the other hand, certain behaviors and attitudes harm relationships. Low self-esteem, taking responsibility for others, neglecting ourselves, unfinished business, and trying to control other people or the relationship can cause damage. Harm can also be caused by being overly dependent, not discussing feelings and problems, lying, abuse, and unresolved addictions. Certain attitudes such as hopelessness, resentment, perpetual criticism, naivete, unreliability, hardheartedness, negativity, or cynicism can ruin relationhips.

- Being too selfish, or not selfish enough, can hurt relationships.
- Too little or too much tolerance can harm relationships.
- Having expectations too high or too low can hurt relationships.
- Looking for all our good feelings, excitement, or stimulation from our relationships can damage them.
- Not learning from our mistakes can cause us to repeat the same mistakes.
- Being too hard on ourselves for our mistakes can hurt relationships.
- Expecting other people, ourselves, or our relationships to be perfect can damage relationships.
- Not examining a relationship enough can damage it; so can holding it under a microscope.

Relationships and love have a life of their own.[5] Like other living things, they have a birth, death, and some activity between — a beginning, middle, and end.[6] Some run the course in twelve hours; some span a lifetime. Like other living things, relationships are cyclical, not static. We have cycles of passion and boredom, ease and struggle, closeness and distance, joy and pain, growth and repose.[7]

Sometimes as the cycles or seasons of relationships change,

the boundaries and dimensions of relationships change. We can learn to be flexible enough to go through and accept these changing seasons.

We've identified many types of relationships. We label some "healthy" and some "unhealthy." The energy between two people can be positive or negative. Relationships can be formed out of our deficiencies, our strengths, or out of loneliness. Some are based on chemistry. Most combine these characteristics and are formed for many reasons — many of which are unknown to people at the time and become clear only in retrospect. Usually, two people simply believe they love each other and the relationship seems to fit.[8] The relationship meets both people's needs at the time.[9]

In his lectures and writing, Earnie Larsen has identified three relationship states: "in," "out," or "wait." And there can be no relationship if one person calls "out," says Larsen.

No particular state of being "in or out of a relationship" indicates recovery. Recovery is indicated by each of us making our own choices about what we want and need to do, and what's important to us. Perhaps no area of our lives expresses our uniqueness as much as our relationships — our relationship history, present circumstances, and goals.

When Sheryl began recovering from codependency, she divorced her husband, who she calls "a practicing sex addict and alcoholic." Now, two and one-half years later, she dates only occasionally.

"It wouldn't be fair to me or a man to get into a relationship yet. I'm not ready. Besides, I don't know anyone I want to be involved with. I want a good relationship someday," Sheryl says. "In the meantime, I'm working on myself."

Many years ago, Sam's wife, Beth, went through treatment for chemical addiction, and he began attending Al-Anon. They've been married for twenty-five years, and plan to stay married the rest of their lives.

"The crazy behavior stopped. Things got better. We don't have a fantastic relationship, but we want to hold the family structure together. Our children have thanked us for doing that. I'm glad we've done that," Sam says. "It isn't a perfect relationship, but it's workable. And it's what we both want. If we had our lives to live over, we probably would choose someone else. But we chose each other, and we're going to honor our commitment."

After three years in Al-Anon, Marianne divorced her husband Jake, a practicing alcoholic.

"We have three children. I was scared about being on my own, and I felt guilty about getting a divorce. I don't believe in divorce. Sometimes I feel sad about losing our natural family. Sometimes I miss the good things we had together. But I don't regret breaking up our unhappy home. It was hurting the children and me," Marianne says.

Jan and Tom have been married for twenty-five years. For the past ten years, Jan has attended Al-Anon. For the last eight years, Tom has attended Alcoholics Anonymous.

"Some days I don't think much of this marriage; other days I know I still love Tom as much as I did the day I married him. Sometimes we've grown together, sometimes apart," says Jan. "We've changed a lot, but in some ways we're still the same. What has changed is this: I'm with Tom today because I'm choosing to be with him, not because I think I don't have a choice."

I've heard many relationship stories. Some recovering people are happily married, some unhappily married, some in so-so marriages, and some fluctuate. Some people are divorced, some single and looking, some single and avoiding relationships. Some people are dating, some living together and very committed, some are together one day at a time. Some people formed successful relationships after they began recovering; some didn't. Some couples are working on salvageable relationships from pre-recovery days.

Some relationships last a lifetime; some don't. Many of us have decided to call the ones that don't last "learning experiences." Unless we refuse to learn from our mistakes, most relationships are an improvement over past ones. Martin Blinder, who was quoted at the beginning of this chapter, writes:

> Most of us, as part of growing up, fall in and out of love over and over again. . . . While some few people fall in love at seventeen and remain enamored of the same person for the rest of their lives, most of us move through a series of shorter relationships, repeatedly leaving one lover in favor of another who matches our ever-increasing level of maturation. Each new partner usually combines characteristics of our previous lovers and our ultimate ideal, representing, in effect, a re-cycling of the old enriched with nuances of the new. Familiar conflicts may reemerge but are resolved more quickly and with less pain. Mistakes may still be made, choices be less than optimum, but by and large we learn and profit from past experience. In the long run, our newer relationships are frequently a vast improvement over earlier ones.[10]

Despite our discoveries about relationships, we probably still know as much about controlling the course of love as we do about curing the common cold. The age-old advice many of us have heard still encompasses much wisdom. "If it's meant to be, it'll be." "If you love it set it free; if it comes back to you, it's yours." And "to find the right person, be the right person." These sayings did not reach the lofty state of cliche-hood without passing the tests of truth and time.[11] The idea that our relationships are about as healthy as we are is still the bottom line.[12]

Perhaps the greatest relationship failure we can have is invalidating our relationship history or present circumstances by becoming cynical, hopeless, embittered, or ashamed.[13] Our histories aren't a mistake. Our present circumstances aren't a mistake. We may have made choices that need correcting. We may want to make new decisions as we grow. We may discover patterns that need unraveling. But we can learn and gain from each relationship we've encountered. Our relationships are a reflection of our growth, and often our relationships have contributed to that growth.

Although some may be healthier than others, there is no such thing as the perfect person or perfect relationship. Much writing and teaching is done about ideals, but relationships don't happen that way and people don't behave that way. The fact is, some people are easier to live with than others.

On this recovery journey, you are where you need to be, and you're with the people you need to be with — today. You've been with the people you've needed to be with to get this far. It's okay to not be in a relationship. It's okay to walk away if it's dead. It's okay to stay. It's okay to want a relationship — even if you've had one or some that didn't work. You deserve another chance — whether that's a chance to form a new relationship or improve a current one.[14]

You can find love that lasts. You can practice your recovery behaviors with the people in your life today. You can improve, sometimes tremendously, the quality and energy of your relationships. Perhaps you've started to practice new relationship behaviors and have already seen improvement. You deserve the best love has to offer. But the process of getting the best from love begins within you.

Indeed, as Earnie Larsen drills, "Nothing changes if nothing changes." And the only person you can ever change is yourself. But sometimes, by doing that, you'll change more than you can imagine.

Let's look at how you can help turn learning experiences into loving experiences.

Activity

1. Write a relationship history. Include any significant people — friends, family members, boyfriends, girlfriends, spouses, et cetera. For those other than family members, how did the relationship begin? If it's over, how did it end? What needs

has each relationship met? How have you learned, or gained, from each relationship?

2. Are you harboring any negative feelings about past relationships? Can you become willing to let go of these feelings? Can you accept your relationship history?

ENDNOTES

1. Martin Blinder, M.D., "Why Love Is Not Built to Last," *Cosmopolitan* (June 1988): 223.

2. This idea was inspired by my friend, Bob Utecht.

3. This gem originated with Earnie Larsen. It is his definition of recovery from codependency.

4. This thought originated with Earnie Larsen. It is my paraphrase of his idea that many relationships were doomed from the beginning because there is no way they possibly could have worked.

5. Earnie Larsen says, "Love is a living thing."

6. Blinder, "Why Love Is Not Built to Last," 221-22.

7. This idea came from Dan Caine, Executive Director of Eden House Rehabilitation Center in Minneapolis, Minnesota.

8. This idea was inspired by Martin Blinder, "Why Love Is Not Built to Last."

9. This idea came to me from Scott Egleston.

10. Blinder, "Why Love Is Not Built to Last."

11. This phrase is based on another writer's phrase: "achieving the exalted state of cliche-hood" — but I cannot remember where I read it. Probably in a writer's magazine.

12. Many people have expressed this idea. It is more recently and most loudly touted by Earnie Larsen.

13. This thought inspired by Nita Tucker with Debra Feinstein, *Beyond Cinderella: How to Find and Marry the Man You Want* (New York: St. Martin's Press, 1987).

14. The quote, "Adult children deserve another chance in relationships" is said to have originated with Robert Subby, a recovery professional residing in Minnesota.

CHAPTER 14

*I am not telling you to settle! . . . I'm telling you
to go for the gold, not for a cheap imitation.*
— Nita Tucker[1]

Overcoming Fatal Attractions

In 1987, the movie *Fatal Attraction* drew blockbuster crowds. The title drew me in. It summed up my forty-year relationship history in two words.

"I can walk into a room of 500 men, 499 of whom are successful and healthy, spot the one unemployed felon in the bunch, and find him catching my eye," says Christy.

"When I met my ex-husband, a raving sex addict and alcoholic, my first thought was, *This guy looks like trouble.* My second thought was, *Let me at him!*" says Jan.

"There's something compelling about a woman who looks like she might 'do me wrong,' " says Don. "I've been recovering for years, and that's the kind of woman I'm still drawn to."

Many of us have lived with this phenomena of being instinctively and powerfully attracted to people who aren't in our best interests. For years I mistakenly called it "falling in love" and "God's will." In this chapter, we'll explore getting beyond our if not fatal, then disastrous, attractions and learning to be attracted to people who are good for us. Listen closely. I didn't say "boring." I said "good for us." Boring is five, ten, fifteen, or more years of living in close proximity to an alcoholic, an abuser, or a sex addict. Nita Tucker writes:

> I'm not saying you should have a relationship with someone to whom you're not physically attracted. I'm saying that you may not always know how attracted

you are to someone right off the bat. . . . Maybe your mother tells you your expectations are too high. I'm not telling you that. I'm telling you they're inaccurate. . . . I'm telling you there's something far more exciting, romantic, spine-tingling, and satisfying than chemistry. It's when you've been with someone for five years, ten years, or forty years, and the passion is still deepening.[2]

This chapter is about learning to initiate that kind of relationship, a relationship that has the possibility of working, lasting, being satisfying, and what we want. Recovery is about more than terminating relationships. It's about some good beginnings. Many of the ideas in this chapter are based on the best book I've read on the subject: *Beyond Cinderella: How to Find and Marry the Man You Want,* by Nita Tucker.

On Your Mark

First, let's legitimize the process of initiating relationships. It's okay to want to be in a relationship, and it's okay to be looking for one. Acknowledge and accept your desire to be in a relationship. It's a normal, healthy, human desire.

Next, consider what kind of relationship you want. Any kind? A satisfying, fulfilling, loving, and lasting one? A temporary relationship? The kind you've been in before?

Once you clarify what kind of relationship you *want* to be in, discern what kind you *need* to be in. The two may be different.[3] You may want to be in a healthy, loving relationship but if you haven't done your homework (family of origin work) and changed your messages, you may "need" to be (or end up) in a relationship that's abusive, caretaking, or similar to past ones.

Our underlying needs will be connected to our unfinished business, and to what we believe we deserve. The people we meet will prove what we believe about men, women, and what *always happens* in relationships. If we have unresolved anger at men or women, our relationships will likely justify that anger.

We can let go of, or begin working toward ridding ourselves of, our destructive needs or past feelings. We change what we believe so we can change what we see.

The next concept to consider is this business about "our type."[4] For years, I've entertained notions about "my type." When I looked for a relationship, I looked for men I was attracted to. I knew "my type." He stood a certain way, walked a certain way, talked a certain way, had a certain look in his eyes, and a certain history that created that look. By "attracted to," I mean that explosive chemistry I'd experience before I even met the person. I wouldn't consider getting involved with men who weren't my type. On the other hand, I'd enter a relationship solely on the strength of that initial attraction.

Never, not once have I been able to maintain a working relationship with "my type." I could make and win bets that any man I was powerfully and initially attracted to had a serious flaw that would prevent us from having a compatible relationship. On the other side of this coin were the many men I didn't notice. If I did see them, I wouldn't bother to get to know or date them. Maybe they wore their hair a certain way, wore polyester pants, or had a beard.

I am forty years old and have finally learned one lesson: It's much easier to get a man to shop for trousers at a different store or shave his beard than it is to get him to stop drinking. My type wasn't really my type. He was my "drug of choice."

"Who are you dating now?" I asked a recovering friend.

"Oh, you know," she said. "He's got a different name and face, but essentially he's the same man I have been dating all my life."

Many of us have allowed this fatal attraction phenomena to control our relationships. Many of us have overlooked people with whom we really could have a successful relationship. It's possible to broaden our ideas about our type. Chemistry is important in a relationship, but so are other things. That initial attraction isn't love, doesn't guarantee love, and usually precludes love. We can become attracted to and develop a better chemistry with people who aren't our type — but really are. It may not be as powerful immediately, but it will become powerful and last much longer.

In a course Nita Tucker teaches, called "Connecting," she gives participants an assignment: interview happily married couples about their relationships. "One of the things people are instructed to ask each couple about is their initial encounter," Tucker writes. "Eighty percent of those interviewed so far (that's more than a thousand people) reported they did *not* feel an immediate attraction to each other when they first met."[5]

It may feel awkward to initiate relationships without being propelled by that initial chemistry.[6] That's okay. It'll feel better later. You may discover you feel more comfortable with people who aren't your type.

"I was attracted to this man. It took eight dates and many talks with my sponsor to see that though I was attracted to him, I didn't like being with him. I didn't feel comfortable about our time together. There were serious problems from the start. All we had in common was this attraction," says one woman.

This leads to our next consideration: *the availability factor.*[7] There are several *facts* that make a person unavailable to participate in an intimate, loving relationship. That person may be married or currently involved in another love relationship. The person may be so recently divorced, or so recently out of another relationship that he or she is unavailable. The person may not want to be in a healthy, loving relationship, or perhaps the person may not want to be in a relationship with *you*.

Active chemical dependency, sex addiction, or other unresolved issues make a person unavailable to participate in a relationship. Practicing alcoholics, sex addicts, and gamblers aren't available to participate in healthy, loving relationships.

Repeat after me: practicing alcoholics, sex addicts, and gamblers aren't available to participate in healthy, loving relationships. People who need to be in recovery from anything, but aren't, aren't available to participate in relationships. Other factors that may signal unavailability are

- being so tied to a past family that the person hasn't the material or emotional resources to participate in a current relationship;
- being a compulsive worker or so busy the person hasn't the time to devote to a relationship;
- living in another city or state, causing the person to be unavailable to meet the relationship's needs.

Trying to initiate a relationship with someone who's unavailable can trigger the codependent crazies in us. The unavailability factor isn't to be taken personally. We don't need to use it to prove negative beliefs about men, women, or relationships. A person's availability is a fact, and facts need to be accepted and taken into account. Many of us have spent much of our lives beating our heads against the cement and wailing because we were trying to make a relationship work with someone who wasn't available to do that from the day the relationship began. Many of us have spent our lives being attracted to our type when the compelling factor causing that person to be our type was his or her unavailability.

We can learn to screen for availability. Often, it can be determined in the first few minutes, but sometimes it takes longer. "Hi. Are you in the program?" "Where do you work?" "Are you married?" "How long have you been divorced?"

While on the subject of availability, many of us may want to consider our own. Are you still entangled in a past relationship? Are you recovering sufficiently to be available? Do you have time and energy to devote to a relationship? Are you emotionally available? If you're with someone you don't want to be in a permanent, committed relationship with, you're unavailable.

Who we've been dating and the people we've been having relationships with is a statement about our availability.[8] Our prejudices about people and relationships is also a statement about our availability. If you date and form relationships only with unavailable people, and if you have negative beliefs about people and relationships, you may be unavailable until you change.

Affirmations can help here. We can change what we believe about the kind of people we attract and are attracted to. New affirmations might be:

- I'm attracted to healthy, loving, available people, and they're attracted to me.
- I'm attracted to people who are good for me.

If we've been asserting scarcity, we can change "There aren't any good men (or women) out there" to "There are enough good men (or women) out there. I'm finding and meeting healthy, loving people." We can change any negative beliefs about men, women, or relationships.

A prince (or princess) is a man (or woman) with whom you can have a satisfying and lasting relationship, writes Nita Tucker. A frog is a person with whom, for one reason or another, you can't have a lasting and satisfying relationship.[9] Many of us have spent lifetimes kissing frogs and hoping they'll turn into princes, or, as one woman said, "kissing princes and watching them deteriorate into frogs." Some frogs are nicer than others, but a frog is a frog.[10] We may forever feel a tingle in our spine when we see a frog, but we don't have to jump into the pond with it.

What do you want to happen in your relationships? What do you need to happen? What do you believe you deserve? You can begin making space for the good by affirming the good, and by taking responsibility for your behavior in the relationship initiation process. Fatal attractions aren't love. They aren't God's will, so stop blaming Him. They aren't necessarily destiny. And they don't have to be deadly.

Get Set

If we've done our homework, we're ready to do the leg-work. We can start meeting people, and selecting those we would like to get to know better. There are three key words in the last sentence: *meeting, people,* and *selecting.*

We're not out duck hunting. We're not out to bag a catch before the season ends at the stroke of midnight. We're not out to get sucked in by chemistry. We're out to meet people. And we're learning to connect with them in a better way.[11]

How do you meet people? Socialize. Go places where people go. Therapy groups and Twelve Step meetings aren't a good place to meet people to date. The primary purpose of groups is recovery. We can sabotage an important part of our support system by playing the dating game there. Places to meet people include: church; sporting events (as a participant or observer); parties; classes; shopping for clothes, food, or "toys"; cultural events; charitable or fund-raising events; volunteer activities; political activities; marinas; dances; restaurants; decent nightclubs; the zoo; trade shows or organizations; single's clubs; and quality dating services.[12]

If we're serious about meeting people, we need to socialize regularly. We need to look and feel our best. That means extra effort goes into our appearance. That means extra effort also goes into self-care, self-nurturing, and self-esteem. The most attractive people are those who love themselves and live their own lives.

Then, we learn to smile and say, "Hi!"[13] Otherwise people won't know we want to meet them. We may have to fend off the suitors and the unavailables, but it's better than the alternative. Besides, it'll be good practice. We'll have many chances to say no — and some opportunities to say yes. The concept of accessibility, of being warm and friendly, may be an obvious one, but it's often overlooked.

"I tried to meet people for months," says one woman. "I would go to events, then stand in the corner like a statue. One day, the lights came on. I was at some gathering when I spotted a man I thought I'd like to meet. I wondered if he'd notice me. I wondered if he'd speak to me. I hoped he would, but feared he wouldn't. It was all the stuff I went over in my head each time I saw someone I was interested in. Then, it occurred to me. Why didn't I just go over, smile, and say, 'Hi!' I didn't have to be aggressive. I just needed to be friendly. I wasn't out to 'get' him; I just wanted to meet him. I did it. The relationship never got off the ground. After talking to him briefly, I decided he wasn't right for me. But I learned a lesson. If I want to meet someone, I can probably do that by smiling and saying, 'Hi!' "

The more fully we're living our lives, the more people we'll meet. The more people we meet, the greater our chance of meeting someone who is available and really our type. We can be selective, but we can select on a more accurate criteria. Stop ruling out people who may not be our type; stop automatically ruling in people because we're attracted to them. Tucker advocates dating someone three times before ruling out.[14] Take the time to find out if we've met someone we want to get to know better.

We don't have to abandon reason in favor of emotion. Someone may "feel" right for us, but if that person isn't available, he or she isn't right. On the other hand, we don't have to abandon emotion in favor of reason. We may think someone is right for us, but if no feelings emerge *after we've gotten to know the person*, that person isn't right for us — even if he or she is healthy and available.

Let Go

Now that we're on our toes and ready to sprint into the love of a lifetime, take a deep breath . . . and let go.

"I'm out looking for a relationship," says one woman. "I am absolutely wild, totally out of control, and if I can't do something with myself soon, I'm going to put myself back in therapy."

I reassured this woman that the process of initiating relationships tends to bring out the beast in many of us. There are things we can do, however, to make ourselves more or less available for a good relationship. One thing most of us need to do is surrender.

If we are unhappy without a relationship, we'll probably be unhappy with one as well. A relationship doesn't begin our life; a relationship doesn't become our life. A relationship is a continuation of life. While a special love relationship may meet certain needs that only a special love relationship can meet, it won't meet all our needs and it won't "make us happy." If we can't achieve happiness in this moment, we probably won't find it in the next. It's called *acceptance*, the blissful state from which all things can change for the better.

There's a difference between accepting that we want to be in a relationship, and being desperate to be in one. Hungry people make poor shoppers. Desperate people frighten others away. They attract people who may not be good for them. They make second-best choices.

"What if I am desperate?" one woman asks. "I'm so starved for a loving relationship. I've been waiting so long, I feel desperate. What can I do about that?"

I'll answer her question with another woman's story. "Each time I end a relationship, I panic," Karen says. "I worry I'll never meet anyone again, and I'll never be in love again. The truth is, I'm thirty-six years old and the longest I've not been in a relationship since I've been fifteen is six months."

Desperation is like panic. Whenever we feel either one, we need to deal with it separately.[15] Desperation may be connected to fear and our need to control. Desperation may be signaling unresolved or hidden dependency issues. Often, underneath the desperation lie some negative beliefs: about scarcity, about what's coming our way, about what we deserve, and about whether we'll ever get that. If we do find a relationship when we're desperate, it may turn out to be one that proves our negative beliefs. Change what we believe.

Apply heavy doses of self-love, nurturing, and self-care. Find other ways of getting needs met. Act as if we're not desperate, until we really aren't.

Don't take rejection personally. Don't give up, become hopeless, negative, or cynical. A key to determining what you really believe you deserve is how you react when a relationship fails in the initiation stages. What does that prove? That nothing good will ever happen to you? That you're unlovable? That you'll never find love? You can feel your hurt or disappointment, but you need to check out what life is proving to you. If a relationship fails or you're rejected, all that really proves is that you haven't yet found the love of your life.

Be gentle with yourself. Sometimes, the only way to surrender is to experience and work through the desperation. You'll make mistakes. You may go a little crazy, at times. But no matter what your age or history, you can find love, if that's what you want. If you're willing to wait and work at it, you'll even be able to find the kind of love you want.

True Closeness Takes Time

A word of warning: Don't go to bed with someone too soon. Going to bed too soon and particularly on the first date, which is always too soon, wrecks relationships. Besides supremely important moral and health concerns (AIDS, herpes, et cetera), there's another reason not to do this: Sex is a powerful form of intimacy. If we have sex with someone before we achieve an emotional, mental, and spiritual connection, the imbalance will probably be greater than at least one person can handle. And, apart from casual sexual encounters (not the subject of this chapter), no matter what people say, one person usually expects something after sex. *That's normal.* But it's your responsibility to wait until you're assured those expectations will be met.[16]

We can handle the awkwardness of feeling sexually attracted to someone without acting on the feelings. Going to bed with someone doesn't tell us if we want to be in a relationship with that person. The intimacy we're striving to build isn't immediate. Get close in other ways first to see if you even want to be close to that person. Let the chemistry emerge slowly. Give yourself time to develop a mental, emotional, and spiritual bond before sexual intimacy.

Don't Ever Stop Taking Care of Yourself

So often we say, "I want a good relationship. Until then, I'll keep doing my own work and taking care of myself." Why "until then"? Self-care is a lifetime commitment and responsibility. It doesn't end when a relationship begins. That's when we need to intensify efforts.

"I can't tell if a person is unhealthy (addicted, unavailable, dysfunctional) until it's too late," many people complain.

"Too late for what?" I ask.

A characteristic of many failed relationships is that it looks good . . . until we get "in." It looks like needs are going to be met. It looks like the other person is healthy and cares. We let down our guard, become vulnerable, emotionally involved, and things immediately change. The system switches to a destructive or crazy one and we stand there scratching our heads.[17] We don't have to forfeit our ability to take care of ourselves because we're emotionally involved.

"I met a man. Things were great, for about two months," says one woman. "Then things changed. He stopped going to support meetings and started drinking. Things were awful for the next year. I kept waiting for things to go back to the way they used to be. It finally dawned on me that this is the way it is. I'd been waiting for something that wasn't going to happen."

It's possible to get into relationships slowly. And we can get out if it gets crazy. It's never too late or too soon to take care of ourselves.

"What about this business that the minute we let go of our desire to be in a relationship, we find one," a man once asked me. "I've been letting go for a while now, and nothing has happened."

I'm not going to flippantly suggest we "Let Go and Let God." I'm going to seriously suggest we do that, *and* we need to also examine doing our part:

- doing our family of origin work,
- changing our messages,
- affirming that we deserve and will get the best, and
- taking action steps to meet people.

Along with doing our part, we need to let the rest happen, in its own time. We need to combine our actions with surrender and letting go. In spite of our best efforts, relationships usually happen when and where we least expect. Louise Hay writes:

> Love comes when we least expect it, and when we are not looking for it. Hunting for love never brings the right partner. It only creates longing and unhappiness. Love is never outside ourselves; love is within us.
>
> Don't insist that love come immediately. Perhaps you are not ready for it, or you are not developed enough to attract the love you want.
>
> Don't settle for anybody just to have someone. Set your standards. What kind of love do you want to attract? List the qualities you really want in the relationship. Develop those qualities in yourself and you will attract a person who has them.
>
> You might examine what may be keeping love away. Could it be criticism? Feelings of unworthiness? Unreasonable standards? Movie star images? Fear of intimacy? A belief that you are unlovable?
>
> Be ready for love when it does come. Prepare the field and be ready to nourish love. Be loving, and you will be lovable. Be open and receptive to love.[18]

Looking for a relationship? Enjoy the process. Do your part, then "Let go and Let God." Have some fun. Meet people, but don't stop caring for yourself. Learn from your successes and failures. Be open. You may know less about who your type is than you think. You may have some pleasant surprises in store. Talk to people you trust about what you're doing, so you're not initiating relationships in isolation from your support system.

There are healthy men out there. There are healthy women out there. There is such a thing as a relationship that works. You can learn to initiate relationships that work. You can learn to attract and enjoy love that's good for you. Affirm yourself and your prospects. Affirm that you deserve the best, and that it's coming to you because if you begin to believe that, it will.

Activity

1. Describe your type. Be as specific as possible. Is unavailability one characteristic of your type? Have you ever been able to have a successful relationship with your type?

2. If you are looking for a relationship, where are you looking? What places do you regularly go to meet people? What are some new places you could go to meet people?

3. Are you available for a relationship? Do you have a history of dating and trying to form relationships with unavailable people? What are your prejudices and beliefs, about men, women, or relationships? What do men or women *always* do, and *always do to you*? What do you believe always happens in relationships? What do you believe you deserve in a relationship?

4. Write goals and begin affirming what you want to happen in your love life.

5. Find some positive friends willing to support you as you look for a relationship. Talk openly to them about what you are doing, thinking, and feeling.

ENDNOTES

1. Nita Tucker, with Debra Feinstein, *Beyond Cinderella: How to Find and Marry the Man You Want* (New York: St. Martin's Press, 1987), 61.

2. Ibid.

3. Based on ideas from: Yehuda Nir, M.D., and Bonnie Maslin, *Loving Men for All the Right Reasons: Women's Patterns of Intimacy* (New York: Dell Publishing Co., Inc., 1983).

4. My thanks to Nita Tucker for something I've always known, but haven't been able to verbalize until I read her book.

5. Tucker, *Beyond Cinderella*, 58.

6. This idea is also from Tucker's *Beyond Cinderella*.

7. Ibid., 42-43.

8. For years, Earnie Larsen has been saying, "Who we're in a relationship with says as much about us as it does about them." Tucker also discusses our unavailability in *Beyond Cinderella*, 50-51.

9. Tucker, *Beyond Cinderella*, 41.

10. Paraphrase of Tucker's expression.

11. From Tucker's course: "Connecting."

12. Tucker, *Beyond Cinderella*, 75-76.

13. Ibid., 52.

14. Ibid., 60.

15. Louise Hay writes about the idea of dealing with panic separately in her book, *You Can Heal Your Life* (Santa Monica, Calif.: Hay House, 1984), 105.

16. Hay, *You Can Heal Your Life*, 124-129.

17. Scott Egleston is the first one that explained this "switch" to me.

18. Hay, *You Can Heal Your Life*, 105.

CHAPTER 15

*I'm forty-two years old and I've finally figured out
what I don't want. Now all I have to do is figure
out what I want.*

— *Anonymous*

Boundaries

I was on assignment for the newspaper when I spotted the sign on the lecture room wall in the U.S. Air Force base in Panama City, Panama. The sign made a statement about American foreign policy on Soviet expansion in Latin America, but it also made a statement about my new policy. "No ground to give."

I'm no longer willing to *lose* my self-esteem, self-respect, my children's well-being, my job, home, possessions, safety, credit, my sanity, or *myself* to preserve a relationship. I'm learning how to appropriately, and with a sense of high self-esteem, *choose* to give. I'm learning I can occasionally decide to *give up* something during conflict negotiations. But I'm no longer willing to mindlessly lose everything I have for the sake of relationships, appearance, or in the name of love.

For years, I entered relationships with an all-or-nothing attitude. What usually happened was I lost all I had and ended up with nothing. I thought a willingness to lose and give everything was mandatory in love. The only place that works is in the movies, and it doesn't work well there either.

Here's the scenario: The man is running around with a smoking gun and fifteen police departments on his tail. He's hostile, bitter, staring out the window of a darkened apartment. His girl friend embraces him and whispers, "I'm with you all the way, baby."

All the way where? A few scenes later, the man is either on Death Row, waiting for his turn in the electric chair, or lying dead on the street. He's gone. She's alone — crying — and the movie's over. It was *his* story. When she finishes grieving for him, she'll really have something to cry about. Besides losing the relationship, she's lost her job, apartment, and furniture. Her credit is shot. Her friends and family are mad at her. And after all the rotten publicity, she's lost her reputation.

The moral of this story and chapter is boundaries. We don't have to be willing to lose everything for love. In fact, setting and sticking to reasonable, healthy limits in all our relationships is a prerequisite to love and relationships that work. We can learn to make appropriate choices concerning what we're willing to *give* in our relationships — of ourselves, time, talents, and money. We can learn to choose to give up certain things while negotiating conflict and working on relationships.

Having boundaries doesn't complicate life; boundaries simplify life. We need to know how far we'll go, and how far we'll allow others to go with us. Once we understand this, we can go anywhere.

What Are Boundaries?

I asked a recovering friend to tell me about boundaries, using her own words.

"How can you tell someone, without using jargon, that you've been allowing people to trample on you all your life?" she replied.

The New World Dictionary defines *boundary* as "any line or thing marking a limit," or a "border."[1]

In recovery, we use the phrase *boundary issues* to describe a primary characteristic of codependency. By this we mean a person has a difficult time defining where he or she ends and another person begins. We have an unclear sense of ourselves. For instance, we may find it difficult to define the difference between our feelings and someone else's feelings, our problem and someone else's problem, our responsibility and someone else's responsibility. Often, the issue isn't that we take responsibility for others; it's that we feel responsible for them. Our ability to define and appropriately distinguish ourselves from others is blurred. The boundaries surrounding ourselves are blurred. People with weak boundaries seem to "pick up" or "absorb" other people's feelings — almost like a sponge absorbs water.[2]

"I went to visit my family. My sister's acting pretty crazy," says Kate. "She's not recovering from codependency, but she needs to be. She's allowing herself to be abused. And she's got a lot of intense, unresolved feelings going on.

"I was around her for one hour and I started feeling all those crazy feelings. It took me a day to get peaceful and get my balance back. At first I couldn't figure out what happened. Now, I know. I picked up her feelings. Those weren't my feelings; they were hers."

The word *boundary* is also used in recovery circles to describe an action, as in "setting a boundary." By this, we mean we've set a limit with someone. Often, when we say this, we're saying we've decided to tell someone he or she can't use us, hurt us, or take what we have, whether those possessions are concrete or abstract. We've decided to tell them they can't abuse us, or otherwise invade or infringe on us in a particular way.

In geography, boundaries are the borders marking a state, a country, or a person's land. In recovery, we're talking about the lines and limits establishing and marking our personal territory — our *selves*. Unlike states on maps, we don't have thick black lines delineating our borders. Yet, each of us has our own territory. Our boundaries define and contain that territory, our bodies, minds, emotions, spirit, possessions, and rights. Our boundaries define and surround all our energy, the individual self that we each call "me." Our borders are invisible, but real. There is a place where I end and you begin. Our goal is learning to identify and have respect for that line.

What Happened to My Boundaries?

"Nobody is born with boundaries," says Rokelle Lerner, a therapist and author on adult children issues. "Boundaries are taught to us by our parents. . . . Some of us have no sense of boundary, others have built walls instead of boundaries, and others have boundaries with holes in them."[3]

Some people are fortunate enough to emerge into adulthood knowing who they are, and what their rights are and aren't. They don't trespass on other people's territory, and they don't allow others to invade theirs. They have healthy boundaries and a solid sense of self.

Unfortunately, many of us emerged into adulthood with damaged, scarred, or nonexistent boundaries. Or we may have constructed such a thick turtle shell around us people can't get close.

Many events contribute to this. It happens when healthy boundaries aren't role modeled or taught to children, when children's boundaries and rights are invaded or violated, and when children are forced into inappropriate roles with those around them.[4] Diseases like chemical dependency or other compulsive disorders play hell with boundaries.

Children may have weak or nonexistent boundaries if they were emotionally or physically neglected or abandoned. Their boundaries also may be weak if they weren't nurtured or didn't grow up with appropriate discipline and limits. They may not develop a self, an identity, or a healthy sense of self-esteem. It's difficult for a "self" to form in a void.

Abuse, humiliation, or shame damages boundaries. It leaves gaping holes where the violation occurred.[5] If we were emotionally, physically, or sexually abused as children, we may grow up without healthy borders around that part of our territory. As adults, we'll be vulnerable to invasion in that area until we repair and strengthen that part of our border.

Inappropriate generational roles among family members, and inappropriate roles between our family and other families, can damage boundary formation.[6] We may not have learned to identify or respect other people's territory or our own territory.

If we had to take care of someone who was supposed to be our caregiver, we may believe other people's thoughts, feelings, and problems are our responsibility. If we lived with someone who encouraged us to be overly dependent on him or her, we may not have learned we had a complete self of our own. We may have entered adulthood feeling like we were half of something, and needed another person to be complete. Caretaking, whether it involves other people taking responsibility for us or us taking responsibility for them, damages boundaries. It leaves us with an unclear sense of ourselves and others — of who we and others are.

Controlling people invade territory.[7] They trespass, and think it's their right to do that. If we lived with someone who tried to control our thoughts, bodies, or feelings, our boundaries may have been damaged. If our rights to our emotions, thoughts, bodies, privacy, and possessions weren't respected, we may not know we have rights. We may not know others do too.

Our original bond with our primary caregiver determines how we bond with others.[8] Our boundaries determine how we fit or bond with those around us. If we have weak boundaries, we may get lost in other people's territory. If we have holes or gaps in our borders, we're vulnerable to invasion. If our borders are too thick and rigid, we won't let people get close to us.

Without boundaries, relationships will cause us fear. We're vulnerable to losing all we have, including ourselves.

With too many boundaries, we won't have any relationships. We won't dare get too close, because it'll be a long time before we see our *selves* again. People may run from us.

People feel most comfortable around people who have

healthy boundaries. It's uncomfortable to be around people with too many or too few boundaries. It's uncomfortable to be around trespassers, although if we've lived with certain kinds of invaders and trespassers all our lives, we may not realize how uncomfortable it feels to be around them.

The goal in recovery is to develop healthy boundaries, not too pliable nor too rigid. And we patch any chinks in our borders. Developing healthy boundaries is our responsibility. We cannot afford to put the responsibility for taking care of ourselves, or looking out for our best interests, in anyone's hands but ours and our Higher Power's.

As we develop healthy boundaries, we develop an appropriate sense of roles among family members, others, and ourselves. We learn to respect others and ourselves. We don't use or abuse others or allow them to use or abuse us. We stop abusing ourselves! We don't control others or let them control us. We stop taking responsibility for other people and stop letting them take responsibility for us. We take responsibility for ourselves. If we're rigid, we loosen up a bit. We develop a clear sense of our self and our rights. We learn we have a complete self. We learn to respect other people's territory as well as our own. We do that by learning to listen to and trust ourselves.

What hurts? What feels good?[9] What's ours and what isn't? And what are we willing to lose?

How Can I Get Some Boundaries?

"I lived with an alcoholic father and a controlling mother. Then I left home and married my own alcoholic," says Diane. "When I began recovering from codependency, I had no idea of what boundaries were. My life proved that.

"I thought I had to do everything people asked. If anyone had a problem, I thought it was my responsibility to solve it. I let people use me, then felt guilty because I didn't like being used. My husband manipulated me, lied to me, and verbally abused me. I felt guilty because I didn't like the way he treated me. My children walked all over me. They talked any way they wanted to me. They refused to respect or follow my rules. I felt guilty when I became angry at them for treating me that way.

"I've been recovering from codependency for eight years now," Diane continues. "Gradually, I've learned to recognize the difference between appropriate and inappropriate treatment. I've come to believe I deserve to be treated well and with respect by people, including my children. I know I don't have to allow people to use me or talk ugly to me. I don't have to do everything people ask or tell me to do. I don't have to be touched when I don't want to be touched. I don't have to feel the way others tell me to feel. I don't have to let people use me. I can say 'No,' and 'Stop that.' I can make my own decisions about what I want and need to do in particular situations. I can stand up for *myself*.

"I've learned to stop incessantly controlling and taking care of others. I've learned to respect people, their individuality and rights, especially the rights of family members.

"I've learned that if what others do hurts me or feels wrong, I can walk away or figure out how to take care of myself. I've developed clearer ideas about what is and isn't my responsibility. But," Diane says, "I have to work at this, and sometimes I have to work hard at it."

That's the proverbial good and bad news. We can learn to have and set boundaries, but we may have to work harder at it than others. To live with what many of us have, we may not immediately know what hurts and feels good. We may not instinctively know what's ours and what's not. We may be uncertain about our rights. It may be difficult to hear ourselves because we may have abandoned ourselves.

To survive living with hurtful incidents, abuse, and crazy behavior, we learn to deny pain and craziness. If we've lived in systems that have a "no boundaries" rule (don't take care of yourself), we may feel shame each time we consider setting a boundary.

"I've been recovering for six years," says one man, who was physically abused as a child. "I'm good at setting boundaries once I realize something is hurting me, but it still takes me a long time to recognize when something hurts."

Many of us have developed a high tolerance for pain and insanity. Just as experts say alcoholics develop a high alcohol tolerance that will remain high whether the alcoholic drinks or not, we may develop a high tolerance for pain, abuse, mistreatment, and boundary violation. Sometimes it's difficult to discern when someone is hurting us, when we're hurting them, or even when we're hurting ourselves. Sometimes it has to hurt long and hard before we know it's hurting. And many of us don't have a frame of reference for what is normal and appropriate.

How can we tell someone to stop hurting us if we're not sure it hurts? How can we identify it as inappropriate if that's all we've ever lived with? To us, it's normal. How can we know what we want if nobody ever told us it's okay to want something?

We have to work at it. We may have to work harder at it than others. We may have to work at it all our lives. To do that, we need to come home to live — in ourselves.

"Boundaries are not just a thought process," says Lerner.

We need to listen to our body to know where our boundaries are. If we were raised with addiction, a lot of us had to leave our body, to abandon our self, in order to survive. If we were raised by someone who was sexually abusive, we had to ignore it when our skin crawled, or our stomach tied up in knots. We needed to ignore our bodies in order to survive.

Then all of a sudden as adults we are expected to set boundaries. Without being inside our body, we can't do it. We need to learn how to come home to ourself again, to learn to listen to our body.[10]

Setting boundaries is not an isolated process.[11] It is intertwined with growing in self-esteem, dealing with feelings, breaking the rules, and developing spiritually. It's connected to detachment. Shame is connected to boundaries. We may feel ashamed when we allow people to invade or trespass on our boundaries. Shame may try to block us from setting boundaries we need to set.[12]

Our boundaries *and* selves develop and emerge as we grow in self-confidence, interact with healthy people, and gain clearer ideas about what's appropriate and what isn't. The more we grow in recovery, the better we'll become at setting boundaries.

- Setting boundaries is about learning to take care of ourselves, no matter what happens, where we go, or who we're with.
- Boundaries emerge from deep decisions about what we believe we deserve and don't deserve.
- Boundaries emerge from the belief that what we want and need, like and dislike, is important.
- Boundaries emerge from a deeper sense of our personal rights, especially the right we have to take care of ourselves and to be ourselves.
- Boundaries emerge as we learn to value, trust, and listen to ourselves.

The goal of having and setting boundaries isn't to build thick walls around ourselves. The purpose is to gain enough security and sense of self to get close to others without the threat of losing ourselves, smothering them, trespassing, or being invaded. Boundaries are the key to loving relationships.

When we have a sense of self, we'll be able to experience closeness and intimacy. We'll be able to play, be creative, and be spontaneous. We'll be able to love and be loved.

Intimacy, play, and creativity require loss of control. Only when we have boundaries and know we can trust ourselves to enforce them and take care of ourselves, will we be able to let go enough to soar. These same activities help develop a sense of self, for it is through love, play, and creativity that we begin to understand who we are and become reassured we can trust ourselves. Having boundaries means having a self strong, nurtured, healthy, and confident enough to let go — and come back again intact.[13]

Tips for Setting Boundaries

We don't have to construct a blockade to protect our territory; we don't have to become hypervigilant. We need to learn to pay attention. Here are some tips for strengthening boundary-setting skills.

When we identify we need to set a limit with someone, do it clearly, preferably without anger, and in as few words as possible. Avoid justifying, rationalizing, or apologizing. Offer a brief explanation, if it makes sense to do that. We will not be able to maintain intimate relationships until we can tell people what hurts and what feels good.[14] The most important person to notify of our boundary is ourselves.

We cannot simultaneously set a boundary (a limit) and take care of another person's feelings. The two acts are mutually exclusive. I listed this tip earlier, but it bears repeating.[15]

We'll probably feel ashamed and afraid when we set boundaries. Do it anyway. People may not know they're trespassing. And people don't respect people they can use. People use people they can use, and respect people they can't use. Healthy limits benefit everyone. Children and adults will feel more comfortable around us.

Anger, rage, complaining, and whining are clues to boundaries we need to set. The things we say we can't stand, don't like, feel angry about, and hate may be areas screaming for boundaries. Recovery doesn't mean an absence of feeling angry, whining, or complaining. Recovery means we learn to listen closely to ourselves to hear what we're saying. These things are indicators of problems, like a flashing red light on the dashboard. Shame and fear may be the barrier we need to break through to take care of ourselves. Other clues that we may need to set a boundary are feeling threatened, "suffocated,"[16] or victimized by someone. We need to pay attention to what our bodies are telling us too. And, as I said before, we may need to get angry to set a boundary, but we don't need to stay resentful to enforce it.

We'll be tested when we set boundaries. Plan on it. It doesn't do any good to set a boundary until we're ready to enforce it. Often, the key to boundaries isn't convincing other people we have limits — it's convincing ourselves. Once we know, really know, what our limits are, it won't be difficult to convince others. In fact, people often sense when we've reached our limit. We'll stop attracting so many boundary invaders. Things will change. A woman went to her counselor and recited her usual and regular tirade of complaints about her husband. "When will this stop?" the woman finally asked her counselor. "When you want it to," the counselor said.

Be prepared to follow through by acting in congruence with boundaries. Our boundaries need to match our behavior. What we do needs to match what we say. If you say your boundary is not to let other people drive your car, but you continue to let people take your car, then whine about it, it's not a boundary yet. Consequences and ultimatums are one way to enforce boundaries. For instance, if your boundary is you won't live with active alcoholism and a drinking alcoholic is living with you, you can give him or her an ultimatum — an either/or. Either that person stops drinking and starts recovering or you move. I've often heard people complain, "I've set a boundary, but Henry won't respect it." Boundaries are to take care of ourselves, not to control others. If we set a boundary not to be around practicing alcoholics, it isn't to force Harvey to stop drinking. Harvey can choose to drink or not drink. Our boundary gives us a guideline to make our choice — whether we want to be around Harvey.

Some people are happy to respect our boundaries. The problem hasn't been what they've been doing to us; it's what we've been doing to ourselves. Some people may get angry at us for setting boundaries, particularly if we're changing a system by setting a boundary where we previously had none. People especially become angry if we've been caretaking them, or allowing them to use or control us, and we decide it's time to change that.

We'll set boundaries when we're ready, and not a minute sooner. We do it on our own time, not someone else's — not our sponsor's timing, our group's timing, nor our counselor's timing. That's because it's connected to *our* growth.

A support system can be helpful as we strive to establish and enforce boundaries. It can be valuable to have feedback about what's normal and what's not, what our rights are and aren't. A cheering squad is very helpful as we strive to assert these rights.

There's a fun side to boundary setting too. Besides learning to identify what hurts and what we don't like, we learn to identify what we like, what feels good, what we want, and what brings us pleasure.[17] That's when we begin to enhance the quality of our lives. If we're not certain who we are, and what we like and want, we have a right to those exciting discoveries.

Boundaries are a personal issue. They reflect and contribute to our growth, our *selves*, our connection to ourselves, to our Higher Power, and other people. Paying attention to what we like, to what we want, to what feels good and what hurts, doesn't take us away from our Higher Power or God's plan for our lives. Listening to ourselves and valuing ourselves moves us into God's will for our lives: a rich, abundant plan for good. As we take risks and learn more about who we are, our boundaries and selves will emerge. As we go through different circumstances, we'll be faced with setting new boundaries about what hurts, what feels good, what we like and don't like. Setting boundaries is an ongoing process of listening to ourselves, respecting ourselves and others, understanding our rights, and caring for ourselves.

Strive for balance. Strive for flexibility. Strive for a healthy sense of self and how you deserve to be treated. Healthy living means you give to people from time to time, but there's a big difference between giving, and being robbed.[18]

I've listed some "tips," but there isn't a guidebook for setting boundaries. Each of us has our own guide inside ourselves. If we continue to work at recovery, our boundaries will develop. They will get healthy and sensitive. Our *selves* will tell us what we need to know, and we'll love ourselves enough to listen.

Ask yourself, *What hurts?* Listen and stop the pain. Ask yourself, *What feels good?* If it feels good, you've got a winner. Ask yourself, *What's mine?* If it's yours, you can have it; if it isn't, don't put it in your pocket.[19] Ask yourself, *What am I willing to lose?* You may have no ground to give.

Activity

1. What are some boundaries you've set early in recovery? What are some boundaries you've set recently? Can you remember how you felt before and after you set that boundary? Were you called on to enforce it? What are the most difficult kind of boundaries for you to set and enforce?

2. Is somebody in your life using you, or not treating you appropriately or respectfully now? Are you now complaining, angry, whining, or upset about something? What's preventing you from taking care of yourself? What do you think will happen if you do? What do you think will happen if you don't?

3. How do you feel when you're around people with rigid boundaries — too many rules and regulations? How do you feel when you're around people with few, or no, boundaries?

4. In the past, what have you been willing to lose for the sake of a particular relationship? What are you willing to lose now? What are you not willing to lose?

ENDNOTES

1. *New World Dictionary of the American Language, Second College Edition* (New York: Simon & Schuster, Inc. 1984), 167.

2. Many professionals and recovering people have discussed this phenomenon. Merle A. Fossum and Marilyn J. Mason discuss it in *Facing Shame: Families in Recovery* (New York: W. W. Norton & Company, Inc., 1986), 76.

3. Anne Jefferies, "Rokelle Lerner: ACA's, Intimacy & Play," *The Phoenix* (October 1988): 1.

4. Some of my definition and explanation of boundaries is based on Fossum's and Mason's *Facing Shame.*

5. Jefferies, "Rokelle Lerner," 1.

6. Fossum and Mason, *Facing Shame*, 60-65.

7. Ibid., 73.

8. Jefferies, "Rokelle Lerner," 1.

9. This is Scott Egleston's approach to boundary setting.

10. Jefferies, "Rokelle Lerner," 1-2.

11. This idea emerged in part from Lonny Owen during the course of co-facilitating our workshop and support group.

12. This idea is from Fossum and Mason, *Facing Shame.*

13. These ideas are based in part on Rokelle Lerner's interview with *The Phoenix* (October 1988) and on M. Scott Peck's *The Road Less Traveled* (New York: Simon & Schuster, Inc., 1978), 97.

14. Janet Geringer Woititz, *Struggle for Intimacy* (Pompano Beach, Fla.: Health Communications, Inc., 1985), 46-48.

15. This tip came from a woman who travels across the country lecturing nurses about codependency. I met her in an airport and can't recall her name.

16. Woititz, *Struggle for Intimacy*, 48.

17. This idea originated with Scott Egleston.

18. The concept of being "robbed" is one that Fossum and Mason discuss in their book, *Facing Shame*.

19. This came from an Al-Anon member.

CHAPTER 16

"Do you want intimacy in this relationship, or not?" she finally blurted. "Sure," he said. "What is it?"

— *Anonymous*

Intimacy

As I've traveled across the country speaking to groups of recovering people, I've done some informal surveys. I've asked how many people are doing recovery perfectly. I've asked how many have a perfect relationship. I've asked another question too.

"How many of you saw intimacy and closeness role modeled in your families?"

In audiences ranging from two hundred to nine hundred people, rarely do more than two or three people raise their hands to answer "yes" to the last question. (No one answers yes to the first; about two in fifteen thousand answer yes to the second, but I haven't interviewed their spouses.)

A few of us have been lucky enough to see what intimacy looks like. Most of us have lived in families where intimacy and closeness didn't exist. Behaviors such as controlling, caretaking, dishonesty, and sometimes the more painful issues of abuse, may have made intimacy and closeness impossible. The rules — don't trust, don't be close, don't talk about feelings, don't be vulnerable — may have made intimacy and closeness highly improbable.

My friend Chad announced his engagement to a group of friends. Later in the evening he asked Veronica, one of his friends, if she and her boyfriend intended to get married.

"No," Veronica said. "We have no plans."

Chad looked at her. "Your boyfriend would have to be a fool not to marry you," he said.

"What you don't understand," Veronica said, "is if he wasn't a fool, I wouldn't be in a relationship with him. I have a limited capacity for intimacy, and anyone who wants a warm, loving relationship has no business being in one with me."

Veronica's comment expressed a problem common to many of us. Most of us want intimacy and closeness, but few of us know what these concepts look or feel like. Even fewer of us have been taught how to have these things. Most of us have been taught how not to have intimacy and closeness.

I used to think *intimacy* was jargon. I didn't understand intimacy because I hadn't experienced it. How did it happen? What did it look and feel like?

I wondered if intimacy had something to do with sex. Then I decided it meant staying awake all night sharing feelings: his guilt and my anger. Once, in a group of people, I felt a powerful, universal bonding with the group. It happened while one person was talking and I was listening. It scared me because I felt out of control. I wondered if that was intimacy. I tried to figure out if intimacy was the same thing John Powell called "peak communication" in his book, *Why Am I Afraid to Tell You Who I Am?*[1]

Intimacy and closeness seemed mysterious and elusive. Yet, I yearned for both.

I can remember sitting in a car with a friend. We were on our way to a garage sale. I realized I had never let my guard down enough with her, or anyone else, to be close.

I can recall walking into the living room one evening and having the sudden and profound awareness that I was too frightened and nervous to be close to my children. I knew how to stay in the "Mom" role. I knew how to take care of and control them. But I didn't know how to relax and be close.

I can remember lying in bed at night with my ex-husband, longing for an emotional and spiritual connection with him and not having the foggiest notion of how to do that.

In the years since I began recovering from codependency and adult children issues, I've had more moments of intimacy and closeness than I had in all my life before I began recovering. I'd blamed others, complained about not having closeness, and wondered if I ever would. But when I got serious about achieving close, intimate relationships, and combined that with recovery, I started having intimate relationships.

Someone has yet to tell me everything I've wanted to know about intimacy. But this is what I've learned.

Achieving Intimacy

Closeness happens when our boundaries soften and touch another's borders. Closeness feels good. It's a comfortable, relaxed experience. We can have many hours and days of closeness, if we allow ourselves to do that and have someone to do it with. Closeness is something we have some control over. I believe it has a lot to do with attitudes — concern, honesty, openness, willingness, safety, and availability. Closeness can be nurtured, developed, and sustained. We can merge our energy and soften our boundaries with inanimate objects too: a diamond ring, our work, a pet.[2] Sometimes, this is okay. The key is choosing.

Intimacy is the great energy connection. It's transcendental. Our borders and barriers break down and we merge *temporarily and usually momentarily* with another. Intimacy can be emotional, mental, sexual, spiritual, or a stimulating and mysterious combination. Although intimacy can't be examined, weighed, or compared, the most profound experiences are multidimensional energy connections. Intimacy is such a powerful connection that it can't be sustained. It's a gift, a cherished guest that arrives and departs unexpectedly and on its own schedule. The moment we become aware it's there, it disappears.[3]

Closeness and intimacy are like happiness. They're difficult to describe. We've either got 'em or we don't. We know when we've got 'em and we know when we don't. Closeness and intimacy happen when and where we least expect them. They can't be manufactured, forced, or bought. They come as by-products of living a certain way. That "way" is called recovery — taking care of and loving ourselves. Recovery makes us available for these activities. It increases our capacity for intimacy and closeness.

"Intimacy begins when individual (usually instinctual) programming becomes more intense, and both social patterning and ulterior restrictions and motives begin to give way," writes Eric Berne in *Games People Play*.[4]

We can have close or intimate moments, and we can have close, intimate relationships — relationships with an overall tone of intimacy.

Closeness and intimacy can look like two people sitting down, having coffee, talking; three people sitting around the dinner table chatting; two people cooking dinner together or painting a room; two people fishing; one person praying; a couple dancing together; or two people silently holding hands while riding in the car or watching the sunset. These activities aren't necessarily acts of intimacy and closeness, but they can be. So can sex.

For closeness to exist, both people have to want it to be that. We need to be present and available for closeness. We have to desire it and be willing to have it. We have to drop pretense and fear, and shed games and protective devices. Intimacy and closeness can involve doing something or just being together, but the "being" is of prime importance. So is "wanting to be together." We have to spend time together to accomplish that.

Then, we let down our guard for a while. We soften our borders, the line distinguishing and separating us from the other person. And we surrender — which is in itself no small task — to the relationship, each other, and the moment. We become vulnerable.[5]

To do this feat of letting go in our relationships, we need

healthy boundaries. We need to be safe, strong, and nurtured enough to be able to surrender. We need to know we can let down our guard. Our boundaries need to be healthy and firm before we can choose where and with whom to soften them.[6]

To momentarily merge with another in the experience we call intimacy, we must be able to emerge again. Otherwise it's not intimacy and closeness—it's fusion and dependency. We need a healthy sense of self so we can count on ourselves to take care of ourselves. The other person needs to know we'll leave his or her territory when that's appropriate. Both people need the reassurance that when we blend territories, no invasion, shaming, humiliation, trespassing, or overextended stays will occur.

For that delightful, exuberant, lovable child in us to come out and play and show his or her beautiful face in moments of intimacy and closeness, that child first has to be found. Secondly, that child must know that if he or she comes out to play he or she will be protected, valued, cherished, and cared for. That the child in us must feel this way isn't optional: it's essential and a prerequisite to intimacy.

Barriers to Intimacy

To be intimate or close, we have to let go, for the moment, of our need to control. Controlling and caretaking prevent intimacy and closeness. They are substitutes for, and barricades to, closeness. We can't be close if we're trying to control or caretake. Controlling and caretaking are ways to connect with people. They're not as satisfying as closeness and intimacy, but for some of us, those are the only ways we learned how to connect with others.

Other behaviors can become intimacy substitutes: gossip, blaming, punishing, fight-picking, nit-picking, judging, and self-pity. These are protective devices, but they're not intimacy or closeness.

Being obsessed with the past, future, or present will prevent closeness because being obsessed prevents us from being present.

Unfinished business, unresolved anger, blocks to our past and thus blocks to us, prevent intimacy. If we haven't tackled our historical work, if our old messages are driving us, we may be unable to attain intimacy and closeness. If we haven't finished our grief work and accepted our present circumstances and the people in our present circumstances, we may be unable to be present enough to achieve intimacy and closeness. Unresolved anger and resentments, either at the person we're with or the people that person represents from other times in our lives, can block intimacy and closeness.

"I had been victimized by men for most of my life," says Jane. "Several years into my recovery, when I tried to have a healthy relationship, I became aware of how angry I was at men. I had never dealt with how full of rage I was at the men who had mistreated me. I rationalized my anger. I denied my anger. But it was there. Of course it was! But I hadn't acknowledged or accepted it. Instead, I used my anger to punish the current man in my life and prove all men were creeps. One way I punished men was not allowing them to get close to me."

Another ploy that will prohibit intimacy and closeness is expecting intimacy and closeness to happen with people who are incapable of either. That brings us back to the availability or unavailability factor in relationships. Active addictions, serious unresolved historical or current issues, abuse, and lying absolutely prohibit intimacy and closeness. Intimacy won't happen with people with these problems or in relationships with these issues. We can wait until the sky turns purple, but we won't be able to get close to or intimate with someone who's actively addicted, someone who we believe is lying to us, or someone who we fear might verbally, physically, or emotionally injure us.

Someone abusing, lying, or acting out his or her addiction isn't capable at the moment of the honesty and surrender, acceptance, self-responsibility, disclosure, and exposure necessary for intimacy and closeness. These people aren't present for themselves and won't be present for the relationship. And, we'll know, deep inside where it counts, that it isn't safe for us to surrender and be vulnerable. Our territory is at risk — high risk — of invasion and attack.

Shame can preclude intimacy. If it's not okay to be who we are, we won't show or expose ourselves to another. Intimacy and closeness require self-acceptance. We need to be intimate with ourselves before we can be intimate with another.

The difference between intimacy and the "games" we play as a substitute can be described in the following manner. It's a "game" when I punish you because I'm angry at you. It's intimacy when I tell you I'm hurt, angry, and want to punish you. But it's intimacy only if my tone of voice is soft and I claim responsibility for my feelings and behaviors. It's intimacy if I'm willing to be vulnerable, and am confident you'll care about how I feel.

True Intimacy

In *Leaving the Enchanted Forest: The Path from Relationship Addiction to Intimacy,* authors Stephanie Covington and Liana Beckett listed three more factors essential to intimate relationships.[7]

- *The relationship must be mutual.* That means both people are free to either stay or leave, and both are now in the relationship because they *choose* to be, not because they *need* to be or feel they *have* to be.
- *Reciprocal empathy must be present.* This means both people are willing to try to understand and care about the other person's feelings. Again, to be willing to enter the emotional world of the other with a caring attitude, it must be safe to do that.
- *A balance of power must exist.* This means, there must be equality of power between people to achieve intimacy. This

equality is never a perfect balance, but the scales must not tip too far on either side.

Another important part of intimacy and closeness is the ability to distance, to return to ourselves and our lives after getting close. Intimacy and closeness are altered states of consciousness and energy. They are altered or softened states of boundaries. After we get close or intimate, we need to restore our boundaries and energy to normal, healthy, intact conditions. We need to close the gaps in our borders and restore ourselves to a state of completeness and individuality. People cannot sustain permanent states of intimacy and closeness. That's not desirable, and it would probably preclude getting anything else done. We need to get our balance and selves back.

The need to distance is instinctive and healthy after times of closeness.[8] The best ways to accomplish distancing aren't as instinctive. Many of us know all about distancing behaviors. They are the same behaviors we've used as substitutes for intimacy; they're the same behaviors that block and prevent intimacy. To distance we may resort to fight-picking, faultfinding, withdrawing, or any number of anti-intimacy behaviors.[9] If it pushes someone away, protects us, constructs a barricade, or somehow creates distance, it's a distancing behavior. For those of us who have a limited capacity for intimacy, it may not take much closeness or intimacy to propel us to use distancing behaviors.

An option to these behaviors is learning to accept our need to distance after closeness, and choose how we would like to do it. Often, a simple closure of our energy and return to our lives and normal activities is enough.

The more nurturing we are with ourselves, the easier it will be for us to handle both the merging and reemerging that are part of intimacy and closeness. Intimate, close relationships require a strong and nurtured self from both people involved.

Mutual respect and self-awareness are also necessary. We

need to be able to say what hurts, what feels good, and what we need. So does the other person.

We deserve intimate, close relationships. Our capacity for intimacy and closeness will increase as we grow in recovery. We need to go slowly and gently as we learn the art of conditional surrender: surrendering for a while, surrendering with limits, surrendering with safe people, and surrendering with the knowledge that we'll come back a whole person. Once we learn to love ourselves, we can learn to love and be loved in exciting new ways in our relationships. Often, the greatest challenge isn't learning to love others. It's learning to let them love us.

Intimacy and closeness may be a struggle, but they're worth it. You've learned to accept powerlessness. You've found a Higher Power. You're learning to own your power. Now you can learn to share the power.[10]

Activity

1. What would you like intimacy and closeness to look like in your life and relationships?

2. What are your distancing patterns? Nagging, faultfinding, criticism, relationship termination, anger, controlling, getting busy with work? What other, more positive ways could you reestablish your boundaries after periods of intimacy?

ENDNOTES

1. John Powell, *Why Am I Afraid to Tell You Who I Am?* (Allen, Tex.: Argus Communications, 1969).

2. M. Scott Peck, *The Road Less Traveled* (New York: Simon and Schuster, 1978), 117.

3. This observation comes from Scott Egleston.

4. Eric Berne, M.D., *Games People Play* (New York: Ballantine Books, 1964), 18.

5. Earnie Larsen is the first person I've heard discuss the concept of surrendering to relationships. I heard it on his tape series, *Adult Children of Alcoholics.*

6. M. Scott Peck discusses this concept in *The Road Less Traveled.*

7. Stephanie Covington, and Liana Beckett, *Leaving the Enchanted Forest: The Path from Relationship Addiction to Intimacy* (San Francisco: Harper & Row, 1988), 24, 26.

8. Bedford Combs is the person who told me this.

9. Some of this came from Earnie Larsen. Some from observation and discussion with people. Much came from extensive personal experience in distancing behaviors.

10. The concept of sharing the power emerged during discussions with Scott Egleston.

CHAPTER 17

*"Do you want an argument or an explanation?" the
clerk finally asked the irate customer. The customer
thought for a moment. "I guess I want an
argument," she said.*
— *Anonymous Al-Anon member*

Negotiating Conflicts

"Mommy, please don't fight with Daddy anymore! My
friend Elizabeth told me when a mom and dad fight, they get
divorced."

My daughter's words cut into my heart. It was sad she and
Elizabeth thought conflict meant somebody went away. But
they had reason to believe this. Elizabeth's mother and father
argued, then divorced. My husband and I argued, then divorced. My mother and father argued, then divorced. It was
sad I believed conflicts ended relationships.

Many of us have difficulty handling conflict and dealing
with problems. Many reasons contribute to this. We may have
lived in a family with a "no problem" rule. If it wasn't okay
to have, identify, or talk about problems, we may still feel
ashamed and anxious about having them. We may feel
unequipped to solve them. If we lived with the "be perfect"
and "be right" rules, we may be so intent on being perfect and
right that we're ineffective.[1] Difficulty dealing with feelings,
especially anger, can limit our negotiation skills. The issue
may switch from "How can I solve this problem?" to "What
can I do to punish you for making me angry?"

On the other hand, if we lived with too much trauma and
anger, conflict may trigger our codependent reactions. The

threat of conflict may send us into a tailspin of controlling, caretaking, anxiety, and denial.[2]

Growing Up With Poor Messages

"My mother said my dad tried to kill her with a butcher knife," recalls one woman. "She said I hid behind the couch, watching and screaming in terror. I don't remember this, but I still remember the fear. I feel it each time people get angry or raise their voice."

Whatever our circumstances, many of us grew up with poor role models and messages concerning problem solving and conflict resolution. We may have decided that we could resolve differences by ignoring, denying, avoiding, giving in, giving up, forcing, coercing, arbitrating, or walking away. These approaches don't solve problems or resolve differences. They create more conflict by teaching us and other people to ignore, deny, avoid, give in, give up, force, coerce, arbitrate, or walk away.

To complicate matters, many of us have spent much time trying to solve problems that we couldn't solve if we lived to be five hundred, because the problems weren't ours to solve. We may have spent years trying to negotiate with people who didn't play fair.[3] Diseases such as alcoholism don't negotiate. They win — until recovery begins.

Some of us became so enmeshed and overwhelmed with problems and pain we became martyrs. We learned to give all the power and energy to the problem, instead of the solution.

A lack of faith — in ourselves, the process of life, our Higher Power, and our problem-solving skills — can hinder our ability to deal with difficulties and differences. We may not believe in conflict resolution. Some of us may not believe in conflict.

Wasting Personal Energy

I used to maintain a naive attitude toward problems, differences, and difficulties. I didn't think there should be any. I was baffled when one problem after another kept cropping up. Why was God picking on me? What was I doing wrong? Why were other people doing this to me? I spent more time and energy reacting to the presence of problems than I did to solving them.

One day, while bemoaning a particular problem, someone threw the classic cliche at me: *Nobody ever said it was going to be easy.* Right! Nobody ever said it was going to be easy. But no one told me it was going to be this damn difficult, either.

It took me years to learn three concepts:

- I can have problems;
- I can solve some problems in ways that benefit me and my relationships;
- I can let go of problems I can't solve because my Higher Power is there to help me.

It took more years to learn my instinctive reactions to problems: denial, panic, avoidance, controlling, fatalism, and self-pity. These reactions often made things worse. I've since accepted several variations of Murphy's Law:

- Things that work, break.
- Some things that can go wrong, do.
- And frequently, things are harder to do than we think they'll be.

M. Scott Peck summed it up in three words in his opening line in *The Road Less Traveled*. "Life is difficult."

Once we see this great truth, we transcend it, Peck says. The sooner we accept that life is difficult, the easier life becomes.[4]

I've accepted another premise too. A. P. Herbert summed it up when he said: "The concept of two people living together for twenty-five years without a serious dispute suggests a lack of spirit only to be admired in sheep."[5]

Problem Stoppers

Problems are a fact of life and conflicts in relationships are too. But problem *solving* is also a fact of life. Learning to solve problems and negotiate differences will propel us forward on our recovery journey.[6] The rest of this chapter focuses on ideas for problem solving and conflict negotiation. We'll discuss the following suggestions:

- Identify and accept the problem.
- Look for solutions that are in the best interest of the relationship.
- Be open to various solutions.
- Learn to combine emotion with reason.
- Don't take problems and differences personally.
- Don't deny an adversary reaction if it's present, but don't assume one either.
- Learn to combine detachment with appropriate action steps.
- Practice deliberate, time-limited patience.
- Be clear about what you want and need.
- Consider the wants and needs of yourself and others as important.
- Separate issues from people.
- Communicate.
- Healthy boundaries are crucial to conflict negotiation.
- Consistently foregoing what you want and need isn't conflict negotiation.
- Avoid power plays.

- Learn to recognize when you're negotiating with yourself.
- Forego naïveté and cynicism.
- Save ultimatums for absolute nonnegotiables or late stage negotiation.
- Don't waste time negotiating nonnegotiables.
- Let each person keep his or her respect and dignity.
- Take full responsibility for your behavior.
- Look for the gift or the lesson.

Identify and Accept the Problem

- Reduce a problem to its simplest form.

Then, begin empowering and affirming the solution. Entering the problem and solution on a goal list under "problems to be solved" is one way to do this. Be specific about the problem. Be clear about what is and isn't your responsibility. If you don't know what's wrong, you can't fix it. If you don't accept the problem, you won't be in the necessary frame of mind to solve it.

Sometimes in my work, I know there's a problem with a certain piece of writing. If I get too anxious and attempt to fix the piece without clearly identifying the problem (structure, tone, content), I waste my time running in circles and ultimately get back to the starting gate: pinpointing the problem so I can pinpoint the solution. I've used the same hasty approach in relationships, and it hasn't worked any better.

Look for Solutions That Are in the Best Interest of the Relationship

- It means that we value the relationship, and the solution we seek will reflect that.

Yes, we're learning to take care of ourselves and act in our own best interests. But at some point, to preserve relationships — and some are worth preserving — we can learn to act in the best interest of the relationship. That doesn't mean we negate ourselves or our needs, or act in ways that aren't in our best interests.

Be Open to Various Solutions

- Good conflict negotiation means eliminating traditional black and white thinking; it means brainstorming. Sometimes obvious solutions are overlooked.

Grant and Sharon both worked full time. They had two children, and lived in a large home. Grant liked an immaculate house. Sharon's approach to housekeeping was relaxed. It became an ongoing source of irritation to them. Sharon believed if Grant wanted the house cleaner, he should do it. Grant thought he already did more than his share. The arguments took a nonconstructive tone. Then, they decided to stop arguing and solve the problem. Grant wanted a clean house. Sharon wanted to relax when she had time off. They both chipped in and hired a housekeeper.

Learn to Combine Emotion with Reason

- Exclusively using either an emotional or rational approach to solving problems and negotiating differences will reduce our effectiveness.

If we don't consider our own or other people's feelings — and don't consider them important — we'll run into trouble. Feelings often motivate behavior. If we ignore emotions and rely solely on reason while the other person is in the height of anger, pain, disappointment, or fear, our efforts may be futile, self-defeating, and misunderstood.

If we deal solely on the basis of emotions, we'll be ineffective too. Feelings need to be listened to and heard. But we don't allow them to control us or dictate our thinking.

Heavy emotions such as anger, hurt, or fear are best dealt with apart from problem-solving sessions. Anger helps us identify problems, but it usually doesn't help solve them.[7] Learn to call "time out" until heavy emotions subside.

"I had a problem that was driving me wild," says Jeff. "I bought a new car, and the hood popped every time I drove it. I took it in five times to be fixed. Each time, the hood popped open again before I got home. I was furious! One day, driving home from the dealership after the problem was supposedly fixed, the hood popped again. I was so mad! When I got out of the car, I slammed the hood down with my keys in my hand and put a five-inch gouge in the hood. That's when I knew it was time to deal with my anger apart from solving the problem. My anger was justified, but it wasn't solving the problem; it was creating more problems."

Don't Take Problems and Differences Personally

● This approach to problem solving wastes a lot of time and energy.

It's tempting to take problems personally. It also gives us an inaccurate perspective on probable solutions.

Don't Deny an Adversary Reaction if it's Present, but Don't Assume One, Either

● Approaching relationships and conflict negotiations with a "win-lose," "down with the enemy" approach creates a hostile atmosphere. Start by asking for what you want instead of demanding.

Sometimes we may create a negative situation that doesn't exist except in our own minds. On the other hand, we need to beware of a tendency to keep the peace at any price; in other words, don't throw away your integrity for the sake of making others happy.

Learn to Combine Detachment with Appropriate Action Steps

- Don't rely solely on detachment — Letting Go and Letting God — as a problem-solving tool. Don't rely solely on doing it yourself either.

Too much detachment may be denial and avoidance. Too many action steps may be controlling behavior. Strive for balance.

Practice Deliberate, Time-Limited Patience

- Sometimes, waiting helps accomplish challenges that seem impossible, despite our most ambitious efforts.

As with ourselves, the people around us sometimes also need time to figure out what they really want and need, and how to resolve feelings. We don't want to act too hastily, but we don't want to wait too long either. That invites denial. Select an appropriate time limit for each stage of negotiation.

"I impulsively committed myself to buying a product for much more than it was worth," Marv says. "The contract was possibly binding and borderline unethical. I wanted out before the ink dried on my signature. While I sat there regretting my decision, the salesman tap-danced in joy. He had just made a heck of a commission. When I informed him I was canceling, he got furious.

"We got into a go-nowhere confrontation," Marv recalls. "That's when I decided to back off. I excused myself from the negotiations, gave him back his product so he'd know I intended not to buy it, and left. I told him I would contact him in two days to get my money back. That gave us time to settle down. Two days later, I called and gave him and the sales manager an ultimatum: either give me my money back, or I pursue legal action. I also gave them another twenty-four hours to make their decision. The next day, they retuned my money. I accomplished more by waiting three days than I could have by hollering for a week."

Sometimes, people need time to collect their thoughts, save face, resolve feelings, or figure out an appropriate solution.

Be Clear About What You Want and Need

● At the heart of most conflicts is a clash in needs.[8]

It's easy to let conflict exist for its own sake. We forget what we're arguing about; we forget about solving the problem. We begin arguing just to argue. Sometimes, arguing clears the air. But arguing isn't conflict negotiation; it's arguing.

Sometimes, we're not even arguing about the real problem. For many reasons — shame, fear, lack of trust or awareness — the real issue gets fogged, disguised, or lost. Certain issues can become "sacred cow" issues in relationships. We may not feel safe enough to state the problem, and how we feel about it. It may be an "off-limits" problem, too highly charged to discuss. We may feel ashamed to have certain problems or feelings, so we focus our anger and attention on a safer problem — a red herring, as some call it. Or we may be uncertain about the real problem. The problem may be an intangible one, such as "I feel you have more power in this relationship than I do."[9] It helps to ask ourselves and each other if what we're arguing about is what we're arguing about.

Until we understand negotiation goals, we aren't ready to negotiate. The more tangible and specific we can be about what we want from any particular negotiation, the greater our chance of achieving that.

Consider the Wants and Needs of Yourself and Others as Important

● This is a basic recovery concept.

When our sights seem to be getting lost in the heat of the moment, we can slow down and ask ourselves these questions:

● Why is the other person acting this way? What does he need?
● Why am I acting this way? What do I need?
● Is there some way we could solve the problem and meet both our needs?
● Is there an underlying common need?

The more emotionally charged the situation, the more we need to stay focused on our goals. We may want to write them down before negotiating so we don't get diverted.

Separate Issues from People

● Accept people and confront problems.

Doing otherwise invites shame, hostility, defensiveness, and rebuttal. These factors set us up for nonproductive negotiations. Our attitude toward people and relationships makes a difference when we're working through differences. Relationships don't have to be destroyed, abandoned, or abated because a conflict or problem emerges. Neither other people nor ourselves deserve to be discounted because of the presence of problems.

Communicate

● Talk and listen.

Sometimes discussion is the only way to get to the heart of the matter — what's the problem and what can we do to solve it? We may not know as much as we think about ourselves and other people. Understanding our own, and each other's, family of origin messages is helpful here.[10]

A friend told me a story that exemplifies this point. One day, after thirty years of marriage, the wife exploded, told her husband she wanted a divorce, but agreed to see a counselor first. During their first counseling session, the wife went on and on about how angry she was.

"And do you know what I really resent?" she said. "Each morning, when he made toast, he always gave me the crust. I hate the crust."

The husband then replied, "I did that because I love you. You see," he said, "I always thought the crust was the best part."

Healthy Boundaries are Crucial to Conflict Negotiation

● The ideal is having firm boundaries — neither too permeable, nor too rigid.

We need to know when we cannot yield, and when we can. We need to know what we want and need. And we need to know our bottom line. Our wants, needs, and bottom lines are important. What's negotiable? What's not?

Consistently Foregoing What You Want and Need Isn't Conflict Negotiation

● We need to constantly beware of the tendency to take care of other people while neglecting ourselves.

That old pattern of caretaking others' problems doesn't solve problems; it creates angry, deprived victims of ourselves. Caretaking doesn't resolve conflict; it creates more. And if we've learned to avoid conflict by forcing the other person to give in, we haven't resolved conflict — we've postponed it. The cost of peace at any price is inevitably high.

Avoid Power Plays

- Power plays don't work.[11] Power plays usually escalate conflict.

Mother to daughter: "I need you to baby-sit this weekend."

Daughter: "You're always making me baby-sit. I wanted to go out this weekend."

Mother: "I haven't been out in weeks. You're gong to stay home this weekend and baby-sit."

Daughter: "If you go out, I'm not staying home and baby-sitting. I'll leave."

Mother: "If you leave, I'll ground you."

Daughter: "Go ahead. I'll run away."

Mother: "If you run away, I'll call the police."

The statement of conflicting need happened immediately in this conversation. Both the mother and daughter wanted to go out on the weekend. Instead of negotiating from that point, they used power plays — each in turn threatening something more severe. What follows is how they resolved the conflict:

Mother: "We're both getting angry and upset. We're saying things we don't mean. Why don't we call time-out? Let's talk about this later and see if we can solve the problem."

Daughter (*an hour later*): "How about if I go out on Friday night and baby-sit on Saturday?"

Mother: "That sounds fair to me."

Learn to Recognize When You're Negotiating with Yourself

- A good rule of thumb is: If you've asked someone three times for something and the person has refused you, lied to you, or promised to give something to you, then failed to deliver, you're probably negotiating with yourself. Remember, once isn't a pattern.[12]

Some people don't play fair. Their intention isn't to negotiate; they intend to sabotage, coerce, manipulate, or otherwise control events so they can go forward with their course
of action. When you're dealing with someone's compulsive
disease, you're negotiating with yourself.

When you find yourself negotiating with yourself it means
it's time to set or enforce a boundary, or deliver an ultimatum.
You need not make your own choice about what you need to
do to take care of yourself based on the premise that the other
person is not going to change his or her course of action.

Forego Naïveté and Cynicism
- Learn to trust yourself, and make good individual decisions
  about who you can trust.

**Save Ultimatums for Absolute Nonnegotiables
or Late Stage Negotiations**
- Too often, we begin negotiating by delivering ultimatums.[13]
  This is ineffective.

Ultimatums need to be handled carefully. We need to avoid
turning ultimatums into power plays. We deliver ultimatums
as a way of taking care of ourselves, not controlling the other
person. Ultimatums are either/or stands: either you do this,
or I do this. Effective ultimatums require two ingredients:

- reasonable, fair, and appropriate time frame for the other
  person to deliver; and a commitment to following through
  with the "or."

Don't Waste Time Negotiating Nonnegotiables
- Sometimes, at the heart of our conflict lies two nonnego-
  tiable, conflicting needs.

We've set a boundary we're not willing to negotiate — no
matter what happens, what someone offers us, how long we

talk, or how much we understand about the other person. Our goal here may not be to negotiate; it may be to terminate the relationship or change the dimensions of the relationship. Some conflicts can't be successfully negotiated. The people may either be unwilling to negotiate or unable to achieve a mutually satisfactory solution.

Let Each Person Keep His or Her Respect and Dignity

- Even if the relationship is ended, be kind to your adversaries, even—especially—when you "win." Avoid the use of humiliating tactics, and shake hands at the end of the game.[14]

We don't know when we shall encounter certain people again, and what the circumstances may be. We can strive to deal with people in such a way that whenever we encounter them, they will have reason to respect us for our conduct. This doesn't mean we resort to "people-pleasing" tactics. A certain person doesn't need to like us or the outcome of our negotiations. But we can give them reason to respect us for the way we've treated them: fairly and with dignity.

Take Full Responsibility for Your Behavior

- Our behavior isn't "conditional" on the other person's behavior. And it's preferable if our behavior isn't a reaction to the other person's behavior.

If we've been recovering from codependency for even a short time, we've learned we have no — and I mean *no* — control over other people and their behavior. But we do have some control over ourselves and our behavior.

We can be responsible for our behavior even if the other person isn't behaving responsibly. We try not to allow others to control our course of conduct. In recovery and in conflict negotiations, we're learning to behave rationally and responsibly because it's the course of conduct we choose, and because it's ultimately in our best interest to do that.

Look for the Gift or the Lesson[15]

● Some problems exist to be solved; some come with a particular territory; some bring a lesson or a gift we need. Be open.

Somewhere between asking for nothing and demanding everything is the middle ground of conflict negotiation. We reach that ground only when we relinquish our need to be perfect and right, and we pay attention to our true needs — including our need to participate in working relationships.

There may be times when we engage in nonproductive arguments. There may be times when the scope of a relationship changes. There will be times when walking away from a relationship is the thing to do. But recovery is about more than walking away. Sometimes it means learning to stay and deal. It's about building and maintaining relationships that work.

Some conflicts can be resolved in a mutually satisfactory way. Sometimes, we can both get what we really want — especially when we know what that is.

Activity

1. How do you usually react to conflict? Do you usually give in? Do others usually give in to you? Do you avoid conflict by denial or ending relationships?

2. Have you ever gotten involved with power plays — trying to force the other person into behaving the way you want? How has this worked for you? Are you involved with someone who tries to control you by power plays?

3. Think about one or two times you've successfully negotiated conflict. By successful, I mean times when both parties have entered into negotiations that resolve the conflict in a mutually acceptable way. How did you feel? What attitudes and behaviors were present in you?

ENDNOTES

1. Again, I credit Robert Subby and John Friel (from *Co-Dependency: An Emerging Issue*) with the "rules," although other recovery professionals have discussed them.

2. Timmen Cermak discusses this in *Diagnosing and Treating Co-Dependence* (Minneapolis: Johnson Institute, 1986), 55.

3. I read about this concept — negotiating with people who don't play fair — in a magazine article at the doctor's office two years ago. I got the phrase from it, but I can't remember the author or article.

4. M. Scott Peck, *The Road Less Traveled* (New York: Simon & Schuster, Inc., 1978), 15.

5. A. P. Herbert, quoted by Gene Brown in *News Times* (Danbury, Conn.) from "Quotable Quotes," *Reader's Digest* (May 1988). 137.

6. This is the theme of M. Scott Peck's book, *The Road Less Traveled*.

7. Scott Egleston.

8. Scott Egleston.

9. Harriet Goldhor Lerner, *The Dance of Anger* (New York: Harper & Row, 1985), 37-40.

10. This is from Earnie Larsen.

11. I first learned about power plays in Claude M. Steiner's *Scripts People Live* (New York: Grove Press., 1974).

12. Michael Kelberer from *The Phoenix* came up with this tip.

13. Earnie Larsen.

14. Christopher Matthews, "Be Kind to Your Adversaries," *Reader's Digest* (May 1988), 135.

15. Richard Bach talks about the concept of problems being gifts in *Illusions, The Adventures of a Reluctant Messiah* (New York: Dell Publishing Co., 1977), 71.

. . . let me never be afraid of endings or beginnings.
Teach me to embrace all of life with joy.
— *Helen Lesman*[1]

Dealing with Fear of Commitment

"I wasn't interested in Greg, but he pursued me arduously," Mary recalls. "I turned down his invitations for two months before he wore me down and I agreed to date him.

"The date turned out surprisingly great. We went to dinner, then back to his place," Mary remembers. "He talked about issues he had worked through. He asked questions about me, and listened when I answered. He didn't try to get me to go to bed with him. We sat up half the night talking about feelings. When he took me home, he gave me a quick kiss. What a nice man, I thought."

Greg continued to impress Mary. He brought flowers. He offered to help with household chores. He took her fishing. He called often, and Mary sensed that if she wanted to call Greg, that would be okay too.

"Somewhere, I passed the line from disinterest to interest," Mary says. "The kisses turned from nonsexual to sexual. Greg and I ended up in bed. I started to fall for this guy, and it looked like he really cared about me.

"Things were great after our sexual encounter," Mary explains. "Greg was romantic. I felt romantic. We spent the night together. He called from work the next day to tell me how much he enjoyed being with me. We made plans to spend the weekend together. He showed up for the weekend, but he wasn't the man I had grown to care for. We sat down to watch television, and I felt like I had an eagle strapped in my living room chair.

"The closeness and good feelings disappeared. I could feel something shift when I became interested in him. The moment I became emotionally involved, Greg stopped being involved. He was emotionally gone. I started to feel desperate, dependent, controlling, and scared. I didn't know what was wrong. When I tried to get him to talk about it, he mumbled something about feeling strange when he made plans, and how he needed to be spontaneous. It took less than a week for the 'relationship' to crumble. He wouldn't talk. He didn't call. I no longer felt comfortable calling him. What happened to the nice guy who shared feelings? What happened to the guy who was so interested in me? I spent a week trying to figure out what I was doing wrong. Then I realized that my mistake was getting interested in him. Greg wasn't pursuing me in spite of my disinterest. He was pursuing me because of my disinterest."

Kathryn's Story

Kathryn was ecstatic. She had finally saved enough money to buy the car she wanted. She had taken months to shop around and close the deal. Now, it was time to go to the lot and drive away in her gorgeous red Bonneville.

Kathryn sat in the sales manager's office, signing one form after another. As she put her signature on each successive form, her ecstasy turned to distress. She felt irritable, jumpy, and anxious. The salesman led her to the new car, opened the door, and handed her the keys. Kathryn slid into the seat. She barely heard the salesman's final instructions.

"I started perspiring. My hands trembled. The salesman was standing right next to me, but it sounded like he was in a tunnel. All I wanted was out," Kathryn said.

She drove the car around the block, then returned to the car lot, ran to the sales manager's office, and demanded that he cancel the sale. He refused. The salesman was confused. The sales manager was confused. They tried to calm her down. When they tried to placate her, Kathryn became more upset.

She walked to the nearest phone and called her attorney. After explaining what happened, as best she could, Kathryn asked how she could get out of the deal. The attorney told her to leave the new car at the lot if she definitely didn't want it. Kathryn hung up the phone.

"The minute I thought I could get out of the deal, I realized I didn't want to," Kathryn said. "What had I just done? I really wanted the car! I didn't want to leave it here. I got in my new car and drove away feeling embarrassed and confused."

Those Two Words: "Commitment" and "Relationship"

What happened to Greg and Kathryn happens to many people: fear of commitment. Some call it a sign of the times; some call it a symptom of the adult child syndrome. And for some, it's not fear; it's panic bordering on phobia.

When I ask men and women what they consider to be the biggest problem with members of the opposite sex, men tell me women seem to get bored and lose interest if a man acts interested and treats a woman well; women complain men won't commit.

"Fear of commitment?" says Allen, who's been recovering for several years. "I see a bunch of people doing it, calling it a lot of different things."

The problem of trying to deal with someone frightened of commitment, or trying to understand our own fear of commitment, perplexes many of us. I used to joke I could clear out a crowded nightclub by walking around to the tables and whispering two words in each man's ear: "commitment" and "relationship." I said it would scare everyone away, but the fact is those words scare me.

A commitment means pledging our time, interest, care, love, money, presence, energy, *ourselves*, or any combination of these, to a person, place, project, or thing for a specified time period. The commitments we fear may be as minor as finishing a project or as major as walking down the aisle and saying, "I do." People may fear committing to many situations: a rent lease, a major purchase; specific plans with lovers, friends, or relatives; joining a church or synagogue; a structured nine-to-five job; an extended volunteer position such as serving on a board of directors; or a relationship.[2]

We might not call our "fear of commitment" a "fear of commitment." We may call it "liking to be spontaneous," "not believing in a silly piece of paper," or "liking our space and freedom."[3] But the bottom line is this: our inability to commit, whether it's 'til death do us part or for three hours on Friday night, can spoil our chances for the good stuff.

Many of us have different degrees of fear about commitment, and we may each have particular commitments that set our hands and hearts to trembling. For some, the fear becomes an intense reaction caused by the thought of being caged, trapped, burdened, obligated, or forever and hopelessly *committed*.[4]

"When a person senses some type of threat or danger, the body has a very specific way of reacting," write Steven Carter and Julia Sokol in *Men Who Can't Love*, a good book about men who fear commitment and the women who love them.

An extreme fear of commitment can actually produce different degrees of one or more of the following symptoms, according to Carter and Sokol.

- Waves of anxiety
- A sense of dread
- Hyperventilating
- Labored breathing
- Suffocating sensations
- A skipping or racing heart
- Stomach distress
- Sweating or chills ("cold feet")

In many situations this response is entirely appropriate and expected. It is not surprising, for example, to experience these symptoms when confronted by a snarling Doberman or an armed assailant. But often these very same symptoms are triggered by a far more subtle threat, even a seemingly innocuous object or circumstance, such as an elevator, a bridge, a spider, or a relationship. When we have an inappropriate reaction such as this, when the body's fear response seems greatly exaggerated or totally irrational, we call it a phobic response.[5]

In *Men Who Can't Love,* the authors describe typical and predictable stages of relationship behavior for a person afraid to commit.

The Beginning: All he can think about is how much he wants you. The Middle: He knows he has you, and it scares him. The End: You want him, and he's running scared. The Bitter End: It's all over and you don't know why.[6]

The fear of commitment can set in at any stage in a relationship: after a good first date; after the first sexual encounter; when it's time to settle in, typically when two people decide to live together; or after they march down the aisle and pledge love for a lifetime.[7]

It can be confusing and painful to date, love, or be friends with a person afraid to commit. It can be confusing and painful to be a person who fears commitment.

Friends may wonder why Harry refused to make plans to go out with them.

Relatives may wonder why Jan refuses to commit to coming for Christmas dinner.

Lovers may wonder why the person who pursued them so arduously disappears, backs off, or gets cold feet.

The answer is that people truly do get "cold feet."

People afraid to commit aren't necessarily "unhealthy." They aren't necessarily uncaring "womanizers" or "man haters." They're people with a fear, sometimes a dreadful fear, of committing. Some of us who are afraid of committing may not know we harbor this fear. All we know is an uncomfortable feeling is present, and getting out of the commitment soothes the feeling.

Getting Cold Feet

The anxiety produced by making a particular commitment can be overwhelming, like the terror experienced by a claustrophobic who has been locked in a closet. Getting out of the commitment can be like the claustrophobic getting out of the closet. Creating distance, getting out, or getting away makes it feel better, since this is an instinctive reaction to feeling trapped. Once away and relaxed, we may feel safe enough to examine the feelings that led to the commitment in the first place. We may discover we really want who or what we've run from.[8]

"Marsha and I dated for months," Tom says. "It felt like we just couldn't be together enough. We made plans to move in together. I couldn't wait. But the day I was supposed to move in, something happened inside me. I panicked. I forced myself through the move, kind of. I brought my body to Marsha's house but I left my suitcases in my car. I couldn't bring myself to move one piece of furniture in with me.

"Each day, I got what I needed from the car. Slowly, I accumulated a few items in the house, but I never completely moved in. I woke up and left the house at 5:30 A.M. to work out. I'd get to the health club ten minutes before it opened! I'd get home late at night just in time to go to sleep.

"Marsha was patient for a while; then she started complaining. I accused her of being too demanding. She said she wasn't going to demand anything from me because I was history. I said fine, I wanted my space and freedom anyway. And I moved out.

"The minute I got my space and freedom, all I wanted was to be with Marsha. I was ready to commit. But Marsha wasn't.

That was months ago and we're still not back together."

The perplexing and painful aspect about being in a relationship with a person who fears commitment is this: The fear of commitment emerges when a relationship is at its best, finest, or closest.[9] When the relationship isn't going well or the other person isn't interested, those of us who are afraid to commit feel safe enough to be interested. There's no threat. A person afraid to commit can only be "in" if the other person is "out." When the other person moves "in," the person afraid to commit moves back "out." Sometimes, the person afraid of committing chooses to be in a relationship with a person he knows he won't (or can't) commit to. Then when it's time to get "out," the excuse is ready.[10]

Other Factors Contributing to Fear of Commitment

Our fear of committing may be intertwined with fear of intimacy and closeness, unresolved shame issues, a previous commitment gone sour, not feeling safe, or not trusting ourselves to take care of ourselves. Fear of commitment may be caused by weak boundaries, fear of losing control, anxiety over whether we can live up to our promise, unresolved guilt over failed promises, fear of being hurt, or a fear of being trapped.

Many of the situations and people we've lived with could reasonably cause us to fear commitment. Some of us spent years overcommitting and overextending ourselves. We may react to this tendency in ourselves by refusing to commit to anything. Our tendency to remain committed to people who use our commitment and loyalty against us, can cause us to be leery of commitments.

"I was so committed to my marriage and my husband," says Darlene, "I used to joke that love was a ten-letter word spelled c-o-m-m-i-t-m-e-n-t. The problem was, my husband wasn't committed. He ran around on me and lied to me. He assumed I would always honor my commitment no matter what he did. He was almost right. It was hard for me to back out of my marriage vows. It's going to be a long time before I make that kind of commitment again."

Sometimes, our fear of commitment isn't our issue. It's an instinctive reaction to unresolved desperation and dependency issues in the other person.[11]

Not trusting ourselves and our choices can make us afraid to make long-term, or even short-term, commitments. Some of us were deprived of enough protection, permission, nurturing, and role modeling to learn that we could follow through on a promise and feel good about doing so.

Some of us have a thinking "disorder" about what constitutes a commitment. Some of us confuse accepting an invitation to dance with accepting an invitation to get married. Some of us are frightened by anything remotely resembling "forever," so one year, one month, or one evening can feel like an eternity, especially if we tend to "get lost" in other people.

Some of us can become as afraid of ending a relationship as we can to beginning it.[12] Some couples get stuck in the never-never land of distance dancing in relationships, afraid to commit either way.

"Karen was interested in having a relationship with me, until I decided I was interested in her. When I stopped balking, Karen started balking," Ralph explains. "We've gone back and forth this way for two years now. When one of us gets too close, the other one backs away. But the moment one of us backs too far away, the other one moves in closer. We can't seem to get in, and we can't seem to get out."

This is the good news: We'll each work through our fear of commitment at our own time and pace. We can each figure out what our fears are trying to tell us.

Sometimes, our instincts are telling us we don't want to commit. Not all relationships are meant to be forever. Some relationships are healing relationships, some are transitional, and some are "practice" relationships.[13] We can value the friendship and appreciate the learning experiences, but we don't have to marry everyone we date.[14]

Sometimes, our fear is signaling that we're not yet ready to commit to someone or something. I've seen couples distance dance for years, then decide, "That's it. It's time to settle down and stop this."

I've seen people refuse to commit to someone or something one month, then change their minds the next, make a commitment, and feel pleased they did.

I've seen people commit and regret it.

I've seen people despair one year because they loved someone who wouldn't commit to them, then rejoice the next year because they see the relationship would have been a disaster.

There's not one way to deal with fear of commitment. Each situation requires individual consideration. Sometimes our fear signals that a particular move is wrong for us. Sometimes it's just the fear of pledging ourselves to something new. Other times, it's an overreaction to making a decision that seems extremely long-term or perhaps mistaken.

When the Other Person Is Afraid to Commit

It can be "crazy-making" to love or care about someone who's afraid to commit. It can trigger all sorts of the codependent crazies in us — from desperation to wondering, "What's wrong with me?"

When we love someone who's afraid to commit, our worst possible reactions are usually our instinctive ones: taking things personally, trying to make him or her feel guilty, and becoming aggressive, needy, or demanding. If someone is feeling trapped, our tendency to get demanding, controlling, or desperate makes them feel more trapped. The best thing we can do is allow that person, without shame or guilt, to have his or her feelings. In other words, we detach; we allow the person to make a choice about what he or she wants to do. Then we concentrate on taking care of ourselves.[15] Nevertheless, there comes a time, as part of taking care of ourselves, when we do expect certain things from people, including a commitment to a relationship. When it's appropriate, we may need to set boundaries and deliver well-timed ultimatums.[16]

If the substance of a relationship is good and it's moving forward, we can be patient. If a person is acting committed, but is afraid to verbalize that commitment, we may want to be patient.[17] It's normal for anyone to have some twinges of panic and a few second thoughts about committing. If the substance of a relationship isn't good, remember that a commitment doesn't change the content of a relationship. Marriage or commitment is a continuation, not a cure.

If we're regularly attracted to people who refuse to commit, we may question whether we're being attracted to their unavailability. Some of us may also want to examine whether our desperation or dependency issues are causing people to run from us.

When We're Afraid to Commit

If we're afraid to commit, the first step toward dealing with our fear is to become aware of it. Strive to understand it. As with all feelings, we need to pay attention to the feeling, but we don't let it control us. Sometimes, merely having information on this process can help us figure out how to deal with it. It helps to talk things out.

"I know I'm going to panic whenever I make a commitment," says one man. "I try to make careful decisions. I go slowly, so I know that what I'm doing is what I really want. Then, after I commit, I give myself a few days to feel nuts. I let myself go through the panic process, because I know I'll settle down."

The key is knowing and trusting what we want, don't want, and don't want to lose. To do that, we must know, trust, and listen to ourselves. There comes a time when to have what we want, we must commit to it. Each of us who fears commitment must understand that as we progress through life, we'll lose out on certain things if we're unwilling to commit.[18]

We'll lose certain jobs and opportunities. We'll miss out on closeness and fun times with friends and family if we're unwilling to commit to plans. We may lose our friends, because friendships require commitment. We'll miss out on owning certain items. We'll miss out on belonging if we can't commit to churches or other organizations. We'll miss out on the thrill of worthwhile accomplishments if we can't commit to projects. We'll miss out on recovery if we can't commit to that. We'll miss the confidence and self-esteem that comes from knowing we can make and follow through on a commitment. We may miss out on a love relationship that could be good and last a lifetime.

Let me paraphrase a comment of the Rev. Robert Schuller's that has stuck with me for years: In each undertaking, we'll be required to commit three times — in the beginning when it's new, in the middle when it's hard work, and at the end when we need that final burst of energy to break through to the finish line.[19]

Sometimes, you may find yourself making commitments that aren't in your best interest. Making a commitment doesn't require giving up your ultimate commitment — that of loving and caring for yourself. Talk to people. Trust your Higher Power. But don't forget to trust yourself too. Weigh what you want against what you're willing to give up. If you want it, there's a price to pay, and that price is committing yourself. I'm as afraid of committing as the next person. It's possible I'm more afraid than most. But I've learned one thing: in spite of my fears, trembling hands, hyperventilation, and anxieties, I'll commit and follow through when I'm ready, when the time is right, and when I want to.

So will you.

Activity

1. Do you know anyone who's afraid to commit? How has their inability to commit affected you?

2. How are you at making commitments? What's your history of commitments to relationships, organizations, purchases?

Have you ever lost something or someone because you couldn't or wouldn't commit? Have you ever had a panic attack after making a commitment? What commitments have you made and felt good about?

ENDNOTES

1. Helen Lesman, comp., *Heart Warmers*, (Minneapolis: Lighten Up Enterprises, Northwestern Products, 1985), October 10.

2. Steven Carter and Julia Sokol, *Men Who Can't Love: When a Man's Fear of Commitment Makes Him Run from the Women Who Love Him* (New York: M. Evans and Company, Inc., 1987), 56-61.

3. Ibid., 191-92.

4. Based on Carter and Sokol's *Men Who Can't Love*, 43, and Nita Tucker with Debra Feinstein, *Beyond Cinderella: How to Find and Marry the Man You Want*, (New York: St. Martin's Press, 1987), 136.

5. Carter and Sokol, *Men Who Can't Love*, 43-44.

6. Ibid., 29.

7. Ibid., 21-23.

8. Ibid., 32-34, 41.

9. Ibid., 52.

10. Ibid., 192.

11. Tucker, *Beyond Cinderella*, 136.

12. Carter and Sokol, *Men Who Can't Love*, 65.

13. Martin Blinder, M.D., "Why Love Is Not Built to Last," *Cosmopolitan* (June 1988): 220-23.

14. Tucker, *Beyond Cinderella*, 135.

15. Ibid., 136-37; Carter and Sokol, *Men Who Can't Love*, 157-228.

16. Earnie Larsen teaches this; it's also in Tucker, *Beyond Cinderella*, 139-41.

17. Tucker, *Beyond Cinderella*, 132-41.

18. Earnie Larsen teaches this.

19. I heard the Rev. Schuller say this in a television sermon around 1979.

CHAPTER 19

Children are gifts, if we accept them.
— *Kathleen Tierney Crilly*[1]

Sharing Recovery with Our Children

"My spouse is finally recovering. I've been recovering for a while. Now, what can I do for my children? What do they need? If we're recovering, do the children need anything more?"

People often ask these questions. I've asked these questions. This book, and this section on relationships, wouldn't be complete without addressing this issue. It's become a growing concern for professionals in the recovery field. It's an issue facing many recovering people who have children. It's an important issue facing our children.

We've established that codependency and adult children issues are progressive. We know that one thing leads to another, and, without recovery, things get worse. We know that many people who recognize themselves as adult children and codependents develop problems with chemical dependency, develop stress-related medical problems, are prone to mental or emotional problems, and sometimes contemplate, attempt, and commit suicide. We know that adult children and codependents tend to have problems in their relationships and other areas of life. We've also acknowledged that codependency and adult children issues become self-defeating habits that "take on a life of their own." We know that many codependents and adult children have been abused verbally, physically, or sexually. We've recognized that each person affected by other people's problems, including alcoholism, needs to find his or her own program of recovery apart from anyone else's recovery program.[2]

Of course, the children need something more. It doesn't do us any good if someone else is recovering and we aren't. If our children have lived with parents with active alcoholism, food, or sex addictions, unresolved adult children issues, or with parents lacking the ability to deal with feelings and be nurturing, then our children may have these problems too. If our kids have lived with parents who have been in pain, then our children are probably in pain too.

They may not show it. They may not talk about it. The walking wounded often don't. They may not know it. We may not see it. We may not want to see it. *But we can know it.* We can know it as certainly as we know how much we've suffered from this problem called "codependency."

Not every child from a dysfunctional family will have troubles in his or her life, but many will. Some will adapt and people please until they bottom out in mid-life. Some won't know they're in trouble until they've had enough time struggling through life and relationships to understand they aren't doing well at either. Some will crash head on at a young age into jails, mental institutions, and morgues.[3]

Our recovery movement has come into its own time. We've come into our own time. We know our problem was painfully real. We each know how much our problem affected our lives. One of these days, and maybe that day has already arrived, we're going to collectively slap ourselves on our foreheads and wonder why we're waiting for our children to grow up before we give them the hope of healing and recovery.

We're going to wonder why in heaven's name we're limiting our "prevention" efforts to classroom education on the effects of particular drugs. It's helpful to know that amphetamines and cocaine can increase our blood pressure. It's also helpful to know that living with an alcoholic or drug addict can increase our blood pressure. When I wanted to end my life, when I was certain there was something fundamentally wrong with me, when I suspected I was crazy, when I lost hope, I needed to learn about me, about codependency, about recovery, and self-love.

We don't have to wait until our children are addicted or in trouble to intervene. We don't have to wait until our children hate themselves before we begin to teach them how to love themselves.

The purpose of this chapter isn't to blame or shame. We can't afford either. My intent is to encourage us to examine what we're doing and change what's needed. Certainly, we can't prevent all children from becoming troubled adolescents or adults. But we can help some.

We've come a long way in responding to codependency and adult children issues. We've come even further in responding to alcohol and other drug addiction issues. But it's easy to forget we're still in the early stages of understanding and treating alcoholism and other drug addiction, and a host of other behavioral and emotional disorders.

We've taken our heads out of the sand. We've stopped denying many of our problems. We've gone a step further and are now actively, and in some instances aggressively, addressing these issues the best we know how. Our best is all we can do. That's good enough, for today. But doing our best means evaluating what we're doing and making changes when we gain new insight.

That's called growth.

As I travel across the country meeting people in recovery communities in small, medium, and big cities East, South, West, and North, I ask questions: What are you doing for the children? Do you have anything for them? How's it working? Are you going to do more? What? And when?

People are telling me about programs that are already operating or in the planning stages. Chemical dependency treatment program staff talk about being lucky enough to have someone in their agency committed to working with the children. I'm hearing about plans for summer camps, school programs that gently intervene in the lives of high-risk children from dysfunctional families, and treatment centers that offer groups for the children.

We have the National Association for Children of Alcoholics. We have agencies like Children are People, Inc., of St. Paul, and Rainbow Days, Inc., of Dallas. Such programs diligently carry the message of recovery to these children who really are people. I also hear something else, something unspoken: *We're on the cutting edge of making tremendous breakthroughs in reaching our children, but there is so much more to be done.*

What Children Need to Recover

What can we do in our families, schools, and communities to reach the children? What do they need? They need the same things we need on an age-appropriate level. The children need to lose their invisibility. They need to be recognized as people who need their own healing process. Did it help us when someone we loved changed, even if that change was for the better? It may have confused us if we weren't given our own help and hope. Often, children who weren't acting out when Mom and Dad were drinking or troubled, begin acting out when Mom and Dad begin recovering.[4]

Children need to know about the effects of alcohol and other drugs, but they also need to learn how to stop their pain. They need to learn how to love, nurture, and accept themselves. They need to know the family problems are not their fault. They need to understand they've been reacting, protecting themselves, and taking care of themselves in the best and most logical way they knew. They also need to know that some of their efforts to stop the pain don't work; some behaviors create more pain. They need to learn about options.

They need to be recognized, accepted, loved, and empowered. They need time to heal from feelings too painful to feel. They need new messages to motivate healthier behavior.

They need to learn about controlling and caretaking, and they need to learn about alternatives.

We need to convince them they're lovable. We need to help them convince themselves they're lovable. They need to learn the difference between shame and guilt, and they need to know how to deal with both. They need to stop being shamed and start being given healthy limits and discipline.

They need to learn how to detach and walk away from craziness before they lose their minds. They need to learn how to deal with anger, but let go of resentments. They need to learn that too much food, sex, alcohol or other drugs doesn't stop the pain. And *we* need to know that if they're already indulging in these substances or behaviors they're trying to tell us they're already in pain. Thirteen-year-old promiscuous girls aren't bad; they've probably been sexually abused and they're trying to tell someone. We need families, churches, schools, and communities filled with healthy people so our children will have healthy role models and adults to interact with. They need to be surrounded by people who are enjoying life and doing their own recovery work, so they can see what the good life looks and feels like.

They need parents who role model intimacy, closeness, feelings, problem solving, fun, and self-love. They need to learn how to break any unhealthy rules they've learned and follow healthy rules. They need to know they're special. They need to begin affirming themselves and everything that is and could be special about them.

We can help them. First, we need to stop our pain. We need to start doing our recovery work and continue it. Then, we need to teach them how to love themselves. We can do that only by learning to love ourselves. Actually, we can learn a great deal about loving ourselves from how we deal with the children.

We wouldn't blame or shame children for their parents' problem. We wouldn't be harsh with the children. We'd do all we could do to make them feel safe, loved, and good enough. We'd give them gentle, nurturing, unconditional love balanced with discipline. We'd teach them about not doing things that hurt themselves, not ever, because they're too special. We'd teach them to develop a positive connection to a Higher Power, other people, and themselves. We'd teach them how to listen to and trust themselves. If we taught our children these ideas, we could be confident they'd emerge as people who loved themselves and others, because the two ideas are absolutely and irrevocably connected.

Once we learn how to give the child in ourselves the care it needs, we'll know how to deal with the children.

"Is there really any hope for families and children?" a woman asked me. "Or are we all doomed to continue playing out and passing on our pathology?"

To that I say this: Yes, there is hope for our families, our children, and ourselves. I believe in recovery. I believe in changed lives. I believe in children. I even believe in childhood. My children and I are learning. It's been a struggle and a process, but it's been a worthwhile struggle and process. Together, we're getting better all the time.

We've been given so much. Let's share some with our kids.

Activity

1. What could you do to help your children increase their self-esteem?

ENDNOTES

1. *Each Day a New Beginning* (Center City, Minn: Hazelden Educational Materials), October 22.

2. This list is based in part on the Charter Statement of the National Association for Children of Alcoholics. The statements are under the category of "Established Facts about Children of Alcoholics." NACOA, 31706 Coast Highway, Suite 201, South Laguna, CA 92677. (714) 499-3889.

3. This fact based partly on the NACOA charter.

4. Bedford Combs talks about this idea.

SECTION V

GOING FORWARD

No matter how it feels, we're moving forward.
No matter how good it gets, the best is yet to come.

CHAPTER 20

"Al-Anon is more than a Ladies Aid Society or a women's auxiliary meeting," she said. "It's where I go to keep on track."

— Anonymous

Working One (or More) Programs

"I can't figure out what's wrong," Jane said. "I feel disconnected from people and God. I'm worried and frightened. I'm having trouble sleeping. And I feel so helpless. What's going on?"

I told her it sounded like codependency, and asked if she was going to her Al-Anon meetings.

"No," she said. "Why should I? I'm not living with an alcoholic anymore."

"I'm not living with an alcoholic anymore either," I said. "But I'm still living with myself, so I still go to meetings."

No matter who we begin reacting to, codependency takes on a life of its own. I suspect our commitment to self-care and self-love may be a lifetime one. We may always need to pay attention to our attitudes, behaviors, and emotions. Regularly investing time and energy in our recovery programs is a good way to do that.

Does that mean we *have* to go to meetings or groups all our lives? No. I think it means we'll *want* to.

Although I'm prejudiced about Twelve Step groups being a good vehicle for recovery, other groups offer help and hope for people recovering from codependency and adult children issues too. Whichever way we choose, this chapter is about our need to continue working at it.

There are two ideas central to working a recovery program: (1) going to meetings and being involved with other recovering people, and (2) working a program.

We need to go to groups or meetings, or find some way to be involved with other recovering people who have similar issues and goals. If we're trying to recover in isolation, what we're doing is probably not recovery. We need involvement with other recovering people. We need support, encouragement, fellowship, and bits and pieces of information. We may know something in our minds, but hearing this information from someone else helps us know it in our hearts. A benefit of our involvement with people and groups is we get to "belong."

"I grew up in a dysfunctional family. I never felt like I belonged anywhere. One thing I like about my support groups is I finally feel like part of something," says one woman.

"But I can't find any good groups!" some people object.

Some recovery groups are in the beginning stages and lack the focus, consistency, and strength found in groups with "old-timers." Some groups are floundering. Some consist of people going to a meeting and doing what they're there to learn how to stop doing: caretaking and controlling. But there are many good groups out there too. Look until you find one. If a group isn't right, you don't need to become stuck or stop recovering. You can voice opinions, suggest alternatives, or find another group.

Finding a Sponsor

As part of going to meetings and connecting with other recovering people, you'll also want to find a sponsor. A sponsor is someone you develop a special relationship with. This relationship entitles you to call on this person for support. If you've been recovering for a while, you probably need to be sponsoring somebody. Recovering people need to "give away" what they've been given. That's how it works.

How Many Groups Do You Need To Go To?

If we have a problem with chemical dependency and adult children or codependency issues, the addiction will always be a primary problem requiring its own recovery program. Our codependency issues probably will too.

When I first began recovering from chemical dependency, I heard much talk about how sobriety was more than staying straight or dry. It meant dealing with all the stuff underneath our disease, the issues that were there before we drank or used other drugs. I've now come to believe the stuff underneath my alcoholism is codependency.

Some people start the recovery journey by going to Al-Anon, then move into A.A. Some start by attending A.A., and later move into the Al-Anon room. Some of us need to go to both rooms. Ultimately, recovery is one big room called "lives and relationships that work." We do what we need to do to get and stay there.

Some people go to one or two meetings a week for chemical dependency and one a week for codependency issues. Some go to a weekly meeting for chemical problems and a biweekly meeting for codependency issues. Some people recovering only from codependency issues go to one meeting a week; some go to one a month. Whatever it takes to stay on track is what we do. This holds true for any combination of issues we face.

We each need to find our own kind of groups and the number of groups that work for us. It may be helpful in the beginning stages of recovery to go to more meetings. During stressful times, it's helpful to go to more meetings than usual. But the purpose of recovery isn't to spend our lives sitting in groups. The purpose is to go to enough groups to get and stay healthy enough to live our lives in ways that work.

The second idea important to ongoing recovery is "working a program." We need to do more than sit at groups and talk to people. We need to do our own work. We need to do our part.

This means applying the recovery themes, concepts, and the Twelve Steps to *ourselves*.

"We've got a Twelve Step group going for adult children of alcoholics," one woman told me. "Guess what? We've found the most phenomenal growth occurs when we work the Steps."

We try to do something each day toward recovery. That something can be brief: taking time for daily meditation, chanting an affirmation of "I love you" when we look in the mirror, or, asking our Higher Power to remove character defects such as shame or low self-esteem.

It requires hard work. We may do an inventory of our lives or our relationships. We might make a particularly tough amend. We might sit down and tackle our family of origin work, deciphering our destructive messages and creating new, healthy ones for ourselves.

But do something each day. Whether what you've done takes five minutes or five hours, try to feel good about it. Tell yourself it's really great that you're loving yourself that much and doing that for yourself. Tell yourself it's great you're moving forward, because you are. Tell yourself it's okay to be right where you are today — because it is.

Some days, we may do particularly well. We may assertively refuse someone's invitation to be codependent. We may deal well with a particular conflict or a feeling. We may have a few moments of intimacy or closeness. We may buy ourselves something special, then not wreck it by telling ourselves we don't deserve it.

Some days, we may have to look more closely to notice what we did. Maybe we took time out to rest when we were tired. We said The Serenity Prayer during a trying moment. Things got crazy and we detached when we noticed ourselves getting hooked in.

On our worst days, we still look for something we've done toward recovery. Sometimes the best we can do is feel good about what we did not do. We pat ourselves on the back because we didn't run to the nearest bar, drag home an alcoholic, and fall in love with him or her. For some of us, that's real progress and not to be overlooked on the gray days.

All the days count. Believe in recovery. Our lives and experiences can be different and better. The process of getting better is happening right now, this moment, in our lives.

Someone once asked me if I was still "in process." I think this person wanted to know if I was still doing my own recovery work, how much of it I had done, and how crazy my life was today, compared to yesterday.

I answered this way. "There was a time when life was mostly pain and problems, and occasionally something good happened. I used to joke about going through ten bad experiences before one good thing happened, and how small the one good thing seemed compared to the bad. But it wasn't a joke. I hurt most of the time. Somewhere, something changed. The record flipped over from Side B, negative, to Side A, positive. I still have bad days. I still feel hurt and afraid sometimes. But the constant pain I lived with for most of my life is gone. And the pain is so far gone that I can hardly remember it. It's like childbirth: it hurt so much I was afraid it wouldn't stop, but when it did, I could hardly remember it."

Am I still in process? Yes. I probably will be all my life, because that's what life and recovery is. The difference is, now life is mostly good, with some problems. Mostly sunny, with a little rain. And I don't know how much better it can get.

CHAPTER 21

*All I have seen teaches me to trust the Creator for
all I have not seen.*
> — *Ralph Waldo Emerson*[1]

Letting the Good Stuff Happen

My friend and I were talking one day. She was feeling frustrated because something wasn't working out the way she hoped and planned it would.

"I work my program. I trust God. I do my part," she finally said. "But how much, *how much* do I have to let go of?"

I thought about her question. I thought about my life. "I'm not certain, but maybe we need to let go of everything," I said.

Let's concentrate for a moment on the spiritual part of the program. I use the word *spiritual* instead of *religious*. Although attending church is an important part of life and recovery for many of us, I'm not talking about going to church. What I'm talking about is finding a personal relationship with a Higher Power, *God as we understand Him*. I'm talking about finding the "church" inside us.

Our journey is many things, but it's primarily a spiritual one. We need people on that journey, and we need a Creator, and a Caretaker to guide and help us. We can't recover in isolation from other people and call it recovery; we can't recover in isolation from a Higher Power, or our spiritual selves, and call that recovery. Our spiritual selves are as much "us" as our bodies, minds, and emotions.

No matter which route we take to recover, the only way to walk the path is unencumbered. Two of the most important recovery behaviors we can learn are surrendering and letting go. We don't do those acts in isolation. We do them in collaboration with a Higher Power. We need a *Power greater than ourselves* to surrender and let go to. We need to know our Higher Power loves and cares for us, and cares about the greatest and most minute details of our lives.

What's surrendering? What does it mean to "let go"? Surrendering is accepting; letting go is releasing. Surrendering is acknowledging the authority of a Higher Power; letting go is trusting His authority.

What do we need to surrender to and let go of? Our past, present, and future. Our anger, resentments, fears, hopes, and dreams. Our failures, successes, hate, love, and desires. We let go of *our* time frame, our wants, sorrows, and joys. We release our old messages, our new ones, our defects of character, and attributes. We let go of people, things, and sometimes ourselves. We need to let go of changes, changing, and the cyclical nature of love, recovery, and life itself.

We release our guilt and shame over being not good enough, and our desire to be better and healthier. We let go of things that work out and things that don't, things we've done, and things we haven't done. We let go of our unsuccessful relationships and our healthy relationships. We let go of the good, the bad, the painful, the fun, and the exciting. We surrender to and let go of our needs. Often, a hidden need to be in pain and suffering is underneath our failed relationships, pain, and suffering. We can let go of that too.[2] All of it must go.

Surrendering doesn't mean we stop desiring the good. It means that after acknowledging our desires, we relinquish them and get peaceful and grateful about circumstances, people, and our lives exactly as they are today.

For those of us who have survived by controlling, surrendering and letting go may not come easily. But they work better. "Surrendering" and "letting go" are intangible concepts that don't mean much until we've practiced them. Then we realize that the concepts are real. Surrendering and letting go can be encouraged, but they can't be taught. They must be learned, and they must be learned anew each time we practice them.

When I began recovery from chemicals, I had to do an inordinate amount of surrendering. I lost a son, a family, my relationship with chemicals, my identity, and all my material possessions. I figured I'd done my share of surrendering, enough to last a lifetime. I was about to learn that I wasn't finished with this business of surrendering, I was only beginning to learn how.

I started believing I deserved good things: a husband, children, a home, and enough money. I tried to believe that my life, including my relationship, was going to work out well. Seven years later I was financially destitute, on the verge of divorce, and standing in my first Al-Anon meeting crying.

I was furious. I felt cheated. I believed God had let me down. I had surrendered and let go. It wasn't fair that I had to lose some more. It wasn't fair that I had another big issue to deal with in this lifetime — codependency. Why? I wondered. Why? Why? Why? Then I got my answer. Rather, I got another question. I had to come up with the answer.

"Are you still willing to surrender? Are you still willing to let go? Are you still willing to trust God, even when — especially when — it hurts?"

Surrendering and letting go are about willingness and trust. They're about having enough faith to want something so much that we can taste it; then deliberately letting go of our desires and trusting our Higher Power to do for us what He wants, when He wants. They're about believing in God and His love for us even when it hurts.

"I've learned that surrendering isn't a sign of weakness," says one man. "It's a sign of strength."

We don't have to surrender or let go perfectly. We only need do it as well as we can, today. I believe in empowerment, affirmations, and doing my part. But I've learned that I probably won't be empowered to do anything until I first surrender and let go. I surrender and let go on whatever level I can muster. This must happen first, and all along the way.

Someone once asked how much he needed to surrender before he'd become empowered. I asked him if he'd started attending meetings yet. He said he had been going to adult children groups for about three months. I told him if he had surrendered enough to go to meetings, he had surrendered enough for now.

Surrendering and letting go are frightening. They feel like dying, losing control, losing ourselves. They are losing control. But then we get back a new kind of power. That power includes, among other ideas, manageability of ourselves and our lives.

I hate losing control. I still try to hold on to things that are worthless on my recovery journey: resentments, anger, fear, and my desire to "make things happen." It's hard to trust. I've spent most of my life walking around convinced of my unlovability. Believing actual people in my life love me is difficult enough. Believing a God I can't physically see or touch loves me — especially when things hurt — requires a great leap of faith. But every time I leap, I land in His arms.

Sometimes, it feels like I have to work as hard at maintaining my relationship with God as I do with people. Sometimes, it feels like I have to work so hard at recovery. But *I* really do so little. It's called "the Grace of God."

"This is what I've learned about recovery and surrender," one man told me. "One day, my daughter got a sliver in her finger. It really hurt and I had to take it out. But taking it out hurt too. I held my daughter on my lap. I talked softly to her. I tried to be gentle. But she kicked, screamed, and fought all the way. I tried to tell her that if she relaxed and stopped fighting, it wouldn't hurt as much. I tried to tell her if she just trusted me, the pain would be gone before she knew it. But she was too scared to trust. When I got the sliver out, she was so mad she just cried and beat on my arms. It hurt that she didn't trust me. It hurt more that she had made her pain worse than it had to be."

Many of us surrender and let go the hard way, by struggling

through frustration, intense desire, anger, hurt, and fear — to that cherished point of yielding, that moment when we loosen our grasp. When we do, something happens. When we stand unencumbered by the past or the future, with empty hands and open arms, we'll find a loving, caring Higher Power who fills us with what He chooses. And we can trust what He gives us, because it will be good.

When my children were young, they loved brightly colored helium balloons. But sometimes either accidentally or purposely, they'd let go of the string. There they'd stand, with tears in their eyes, watching their precious balloon fly high into the heavens until it disappeared from sight.

When that happened, I'd tell them a story.

"Don't cry," I'd say. "God's up there. And you know what? He catches every balloon you let go of. He's keeping all of them just for you. Someday, when you get to heaven, you'll get every one back."

My children are older now; so am I. But we still believe God's saving our balloons for us.

And I believe God catches all our balloons too — each one we let go of. Only we don't have to wait until we get to heaven to get them back. The best and most perfect of our balloons, the ones just right for us, He gives back as soon as we're ready to accept them. Sometimes, He gives back better ones than we let go of.

That's the secret to letting the good stuff happen.

It's connected to our deepest beliefs about what we deserve. It's connected to God's absolute, unconditional love for each of us. It's connected to our desire and His desire that we be and have the best possible. It's connected to our willingness to let go.

Wouldn't it be easier to skip this whole business? If we can't hang on to our desires, wouldn't it be simpler not to acknowledge them in the first place?

Probably. But it doesn't work that way. There's something magical and necessary about the process, the way it stands.

The victory, joy, and growth aren't achieved by avoiding. The rewards come by overcoming. Each time we surrender, each time we let go, we'll be propelled forward on our journey. We'll be moved to a deeper level of play.

Discoveries along the Recovery Path

We've covered much ground in this book, but we'll cover a lot of territory in our recoveries too. We'll take detours. We'll take shortcuts that turn into "longcuts."[3] And sometimes we'll stop to rest.

We'll go to extremes. "I spent the first thirty years of my life taking care of everyone around me," says one woman. "Then, for a while, I refused to even sew a button on a shirt for someone!" We may have spent years hurling ourselves headlong into relationships with no forethought; then, for a while, we hold a microscope over everyone we meet. That's okay. That's how we grow. The goal of recovery is achieving balance, but most of us reach that middle ground only by exploring the peaks and valleys.

No matter how it feels, we're moving forward. And the further we travel, the more we rely on the concepts we learned at the beginning of our journey, the basics of self-care. The important idea is that we make ourselves available to the recovery process and participate in it as best we can, one day at a time. If we do, recovery will work for us. We'll see that all the parts and pieces of our lives weave together in a perfect design.

Some of our greatest mistakes may become crucially beneficial parts of our lives. Some of our codependent character traits may become the basis for some of our finest characteristics. We may find that our ability to be responsible will qualify us for positions of leadership. We may discover that our ability to put up with deprivation enables us to accomplish something extraordinary that couldn't be accomplished without the ability to delay gratification. We may find that healing from our pain helps others heal from theirs.

Let me close this chapter with a quote from Ellen Goodman, my favorite columnist. Goodman shared the following story with a college graduation class.

Eighty percent of life is showing up. Day by day, year by year we were presented with choices and made them. We showed up. And up. And up.

Some are paralyzed by choices. But there is much uncertainty about the decisions that start narrowing options, whether career options or love options.

The twenty-fifth class reunion reports are full of our 'mistakes.' Our lives are littered with mid-course corrections. A full half of us divorced. Many of the women have had career paths that look like games of Chutes and Ladders. We have changed directions and priorities again and again. But our 'mistakes' became crucial parts, sometimes the best parts, of the lives we have made.

How do you make a life? Put one foot in front of the other. Make some choices. Take some chances.[4]

I know, I know. You don't want to make the same mistakes again. You don't want to lose yourself *that much* again. That's a healthy fear, but don't let it stop you from living and loving. You may have been burned from getting too close to the fire, but getting close to the fire is the only way to get warm.

Surrender to the pain. Then learn to surrender to the good. It's there and more is on the way. Love God. Love Family. Love what you do. Love people, and learn to let them love you. And always keep loving yourself.

No matter how good it gets, the best is yet to come.

ENDNOTES

1. Ralph Waldo Emerson, "Quotable Quotes," *Reader's Digest* (March 1988).

2. Louise Hay discusses the concept of releasing, or letting go, of everything. She's the first person I heard mention the concept of letting go of our need to be in destructive relationships, and the more general concept of letting go of our underlying, destructive needs.

3. My friend Bob Utecht told me about "longcuts."

4. This is an excerpt from Ellen Goodman's column in the *St. Paul Pioneer Press Dispatch* (10 June 1988): 14A.

Epilogue

And the greatest of these is love . . .
— 1 Cor. 14:13 The Living Bible

Several reasons compelled me to write this book. It seemed a logical next step in my writing career. I have an interest in this field, and wanted to be part of the growing movement of help and hope for recovery from codependency and adult children issues. I thought I had a few things to say. And I wanted to. I had a dream, a vision, for this book. It was "today's work" for me.

But there was another reason too. On Valentine's Day, 1986, I submitted to my publisher the manuscript for what was to become *Codependent No More*. That date turned out to be appropriate. I've been writing since 1979. I've written many types of pieces to many different audiences. In all my writing, I've strived to write warmly and personally. But never in my writing career have I felt the overwhelming and heart-warming connection I've experienced with you, my readers.

I believe we've developed a relationship. I believe the connection I feel is love. I wrote this book to maintain our relationship. I wanted to spend some more time with you.

Thank you for letting me back into your lives. Thank you for the success you've given me.

May God bless you richly.

Melody

BIBLIOGRAPHY

BOOKS

Al-Anon's Twelve Steps & Twelve Traditions. New York: Al-Anon Family Group Headquarters, Inc., 1981.

Beattie, Melody. *Codependent No More*. Center City, Minn.: Hazelden Educational Materials, 1987.

Berne, Eric, M.D. *What Do You Say After You Say Hello*. New York: Bantam Books, 1971.

——. *Games People Play*. New York: Ballantine Books, 1987.

Bissell, Le Claire, M.D., and James E. Royce. *Ethics For Addiction Professionals*. Center City, Minn.: Hazelden Educational Materials, 1987.

Brandon, Nathaniel. *How to Raise Your Self-Esteem*. New York: Bantam Books, 1987.

Carter, Steven, and Julia Sokol. *Men Who Can't Love: When a Man's Fear Makes Him Run from Commitment*. New York: M. Evans & Company, Inc., 1987.

Cermak, Timmen L., M.D. *Diagnosing and Treating Co-Dependence*. Minneapolis: Johnson Institute, 1986.

——. *A Time to Heal: The Road to Recovery for Adult Children of Alcoholics*. Los Angeles: J. P. Tarcher, Inc., 1988.

Covington, Stephanie, and Liana Beckett. *Leaving The Enchanted Forest*. San Francisco: Harper & Row, 1988.

Cowan, Connell, and Melvyn Kinder. *Smart Women—Foolish Choices*. New York: Signet Books, 1986.

Each Day a New Beginning. Center City, Minn.: Hazelden Educational Materials, 1982.

Fisher, Roger, and Scott Brown. *Getting Together*. Boston: Houghton Mifflin Co., 1988.

Forward, Susan, and Joan Torres. *Men Who Hate Women—The Women Who Love Them*. New York: Bantam Books, 1986.

Fossum, Merle A., and Marilyn J. Mason. *Facing Shame*. New York: W. W. Norton and Company, 1986.

Harris, Amy Bjork, and Thomas A. Harris. *Staying O.K.*
New York: Harper & Row, 1985.

Hay, Louise L. *You Can Heal Yourself.* Santa Monica, Calif.:
Hay House, 1984.

Larsen, Earnie. *Stage II Recovery—Life Beyond Addiction.*
Minneapolis: Winston Press, 1985.

Lerner, Harriet Goldhor. *The Dance of Anger.* New York:
Harper & Row, 1986.

Lesman, Helen. *Heart Warmers.* Minneapolis: Lighten Up
Enterprises, 1985.

Lindberg, Anne Morrow. *Gift from the Sea.* New York:
Pantheon Books, 1975.

Mornwell, Pierre, M.D. *Passive Men—Wild Women.* New
York: Ballantine Books, 1980.

Nir, Yehuda, M.D., and Bonnie Maslin. *Loving Men for All
the Right Reasons: Women's Patterns of Intimacy.* New York:
Dell Publishing Company, Inc., 1983.

Norwood, Robin. *Women Who Love Too Much.* New York:
Pocket Books, 1985.

Peck, M. Scott, M.D. *The Road Less Traveled.* New York:
Simon & Schuster, 1978.

Powell, John. *Why Am I Afraid to Tell You Who I Am?* Allen,
Tex.: Argus Communications, 1969.

Rosellini, Gayle, and Mark Worden. *Of Course You're
Angry.* Center City, Minn.: Hazelden Educational
Materials, 1985.

____. *Here Comes the Sun: Dealing with Depression.* Center
City, Minn.: Hazelden Educational Materials, 1987.

Rubin, Theodore Isaac, M.D. *Compassion & Self Hate.* New
York: Macmillan Publishing Company, 1986.

Russell, A. J. *God Calling.* Old Tappen, N.J.: Fleming H.
Revell Company, 1984.

Schaef, Anne Wilson. *Co-Dependence: Misunderstood—
Mistreated.* Minneapolis: Winston Press, 1986.

Schuller, Robert H. *Be Happy—You Are Loved.* Nashville:
Thomas Nelson Inc 1986.

Siegel, Bernie S., M.D. *Love, Medicine, and Miracles,* New York: Harper & Row/Perennial, 1986.

Smith, Marcell J. *When I Say No I Feel Guilty.* New York: Bantam Books, 1975.

Steiner, Claude M. *Scripts People Live.* New York: Grove Press, 1974.

The Living Bible. Wheaton, Ill.: Tyndale House Publications, 1971.

Trina, Paulus. *Hope For the Flowers.* New York: Paulest Press, 1972.

Tucker, Nita, and Debra Feinstein. *Beyond Cinderella—How to Find and Marry the Man You Want.* New York; St. Martin Press, 1987.

Walker, Alice. *The Color Purple.* New York: Simon & Schuster, 1985.

Webster's New World Dictionary of the American Language. New York: Simon & Schuster, 1984.

Woititz, Janet Geringer. *Struggle for Intimacy.* Pompano Beach, Fla.: Health Communications, 1985.

PAMPHLETS

Beattie, Melody. *Denial.* Center City, Minn.: Hazelden Educational Materials, 1986.

Shame. Center City, Minn.: Hazelden Educational Materials, 1981.

Stephanie, E. *Shame Faced.* Center City, Minn.: Hazelden Educational Materials, 1986.

ARTICLES

Blinder, Martin, M.D. "Why Love Is Not Built To Last." *Cosmopolitan* 204 (June 1988).

Block, Lawrence. "Messages For Your Most Important Reader." *Writer's Digest* (June 1988): 68.

Emerson, Ralph Waldo. "Quotation Quotes." *Reader's Digest* 132 (March 1988).

Ginott, Haim. "Quotable Quotes." *Reader's Digest* (June 1988).

Goodman, Ellen. "To Graduates—March On, Make Mistakes." *St. Paul Pioneer Press and Dispatch* (10 June 1988): 14A.

Herbert, A. P. "Quotable Quotes." *Reader's Digest* (May 1988): 137.

Jefferies, Anne. "Rokelle Lerner: ACA'S, Intimacy & Play." *The Phoenix* (October 1988): 1.

Leerhsen, Charles, with Tessa Namuth. "Alcohol and the Family." *Newsweek* (18 January 1988).

Matthews, Christopher. "Be Kind to Your Adversaries." *Reader's Digest* (May 1988): 135.

Subby, Robert. "Inside the Chemically Dependent Marriage: Denial & Manipulations." *Co-Dependency—An Emerging Issue*. Pompano Beach, Fla.: Health Communications, Inc., 1984.

HAZELDEN INFORMATION AND EDUCATIONAL SERVICES is a division of the Hazelden Foundation, a not-for-profit organization. Since 1949, Hazelden has been a leader in promoting the dignity and treatment of people afflicted with the disease of chemical dependency.

The mission of the foundation is to improve the quality of life for individuals, families, and communities by providing a national continuum of information, education, and recovery services that are widely accessible; to advance the field through research and training; and to improve our quality and effectiveness through continuous improvement and innovation.

Stemming from that, the mission of this division is to provide quality information and support to people wherever they may be in their personal journey—from education and early intervention, through treatment and recovery, to personal and spiritual growth.

Although our treatment programs do not necessarily use everything Hazelden publishes, our bibliotherapeutic materials support our mission and the Twelve Step philosophy upon which it is based. We encourage your comments and feedback.

The headquarters of the Hazelden Foundation are in Center City, Minnesota. Additional treatment facilities are located in Chicago, Illinois; New York, New York; Plymouth, Minnesota; St. Paul, Minnesota; and West Palm Beach, Florida. At these sites, we provide a continuum of care for men and women of all ages. Our Plymouth facility is designed specifically for youth and families.

For more information on Hazelden, please call **1-800-257-7800**. Or you may access our World Wide Web site on the Internet at **http://www.hazelden.org**.

Other titles that will interest you . . .

Codependent No More
by Melody Beattie
The definitive book about codependency, this book is for everyone who has suffered the torment of loving too much. Melody Beattie explains what codependency is, what it isn't, who's got it, and how to move beyond it. 208 pp.
Order No. 5014

The Language of Letting Go
Daily Meditations on Codependency
by Melody Beattie
When you struggle with the core issues of codependency—denial, powerlessness, spirituality, and letting go—Melody Beattie offers a helping hand. She brings her personal experience to the process of daily meditation in these 366 reflections. If you loved *Codependent No More*, you'll want Melody with you as you face each day's lessons, friendships, risks, and emotions. 358 pp.
Order No. 5076

Worthy of Love
Meditations on Loving Ourselves and Others
by Karen Casey, illustrations by David Spohn
These weekly meditations offer insights and inspirations that can serve as guideposts to self-awareness, helping us find the courage to be honest and vulnerable with those from whom we seek healthy love. 106 pp.
Order No. 5005

For price and order information, or a free catalog, please call our Telephone Representatives.

HAZELDEN

1-800-328-0098
(24-Hour Toll Free.
U.S., Canada, and the
Virgin Islands)

1-651-213-4000
(Outside the U.S.
and Canada)

1-651-257-1331
(24-Hour FAX)

Pleasant Valley Road • P.O. Box 176 • Center City, MN 55012-0176